By the Editors of Best Recipes

Best Recipes

CASSEROLES,
STEWS, SOUPS & MORE

COOKBOOK

SMITHMARK

Microwave ovens vary in wattage and power output; cooking times given with microwave directions in this book may need to be adjusted.

By the Editors of Best Recipes

Best Recipes

CASSEROLES, STEWS, SOUPS & MORE

COOKBOOK

GREAT
BEEF

Quick and Easy Tamale Pie

- ½ **pound ground beef**
- ¼ **cup sliced green onions**
- 2 **envelopes LIPTON® Tomato Cup-A-Soup Instant Soup**
- ½ **cup water**
- 1 **can (7 ounces) whole kernel corn, drained**
- 2 **tablespoons chopped pitted ripe olives (optional)**
- ¼ **teaspoon chili powder**
- 3 **slices (¾ ounce each) American cheese, halved**
- 2 **corn muffins, cut into ½-inch cubes**

In medium skillet, brown ground beef with green onions. Stir in instant tomato soup mix, water, corn, olives and chili powder until well blended; heat through. Place in 1-quart casserole. Top with cheese, then evenly spread muffin cubes over cheese. Bake at 350°F for 5 to 10 minutes or until cheese is melted.   *Makes 2 servings*

Microwave Directions: In shallow microwave-safe 1-quart casserole, microwave ground beef with green onions, covered, at HIGH (Full Power) 2½ minutes or until beef is no longer pink, stirring once. Stir in instant tomato soup mix, water, corn, olives and chili powder until well blended. Top with cheese, then evenly spread muffin cubes over cheese. Microwave at HIGH 5 minutes or until heated through and cheese is melted, turning casserole once.

Quick and Easy Tamale Pie

Mandarin Beef

- 1 pound beef flank steak
- 3 tablespoons lite soy sauce, divided
- 6 teaspoons vegetable oil, divided
- 1 tablespoon cornstarch
- 3 teaspoons brown sugar, divided
- ¼ pound green beans, cut diagonally into 2-inch pieces
- 1 package (10 ounces) frozen asparagus,* defrosted and cut diagonally into 2-inch pieces
- ¼ pound mushrooms, sliced
- 2 tablespoons dry sherry
- 6 green onions, cut into 2-inch slivers
- ½ teaspoon Oriental dark roasted sesame oil**

Cut beef flank steak lengthwise in half. Cut steak across the grain into ⅛-inch-thick strips. Combine 1 tablespoon of the soy sauce, 1 teaspoon oil, the cornstarch and 1 teaspoon of the sugar; pour over beef strips and marinate 30 minutes. Heat nonstick frying pan over medium heat; add remaining 5 teaspoons oil. Stir-fry green beans 3 to 4 minutes in oil; add asparagus and mushrooms and cook 2 minutes. Remove vegetables; keep warm. Combine sherry, remaining 2 tablespoons soy sauce and 2 teaspoons sugar;

*Twelve ounces fresh asparagus may be substituted. Cut into 2-inch diagonal pieces; blanch 2 minutes before stir-frying.
**Dark sesame oil may be found in the imported (oriental) section of the supermarket or in specialty stores.

reserve. Stir-fry beef (⅓ at a time) 2 to 3 minutes; reserve. Return beef, vegetables and sherry mixture to frying pan and heat through. Stir in green onions. Add sesame oil and stir. Serve immediately.   *Makes 4 servings*

Preparation time: 15 minutes
Marinating time: 30 minutes
Cooking time: 15 minutes
Favorite recipe from **National Live Stock and Meat Board**

Mandarin Beef

Zesty Beef Stroganoff

1 (1- to 1¼-pound) sirloin
    steak, cut into ⅛-inch
    strips
¼ cup margarine or butter
8 ounces fresh mushrooms,
    sliced (about 2 cups)
½ cup sliced onion
1 clove garlic, finely
    chopped
2 tablespoons flour
1 cup water
3 tablespoons REALEMON®
    Lemon Juice from
    Concentrate
3 tablespoons dry red wine
2 teaspoons WYLER'S® or
    STEERO® Beef-Flavor
    Instant Bouillon
¼ teaspoon pepper
1 (8-ounce) container
    BORDEN® or MEADOW
    GOLD® Sour Cream, at
    room temperature
    CREAMETTE® Egg Noodles,
    cooked as package
    directs
    Chopped parsley

In large skillet, over medium-high heat, brown sirloin in margarine; remove from pan. In same skillet, cook and stir mushrooms, onion and garlic until tender; stir in flour. Add water, ReaLemon® brand, wine, bouillon and pepper; cook and stir until slightly thickened. Stir in sour cream then meat; heat through. *Do not boil.* Serve on noodles; garnish with parsley. Refrigerate leftovers.

Makes 4 servings

Zesty Beef Stroganoff

Southwest Pot Roast

¼ cup all-purpose flour
2 teaspoons garlic salt
½ teaspoon ground red
    pepper
4 to 5 pounds boneless beef
    rump roast
1 tablespoon vegetable oil
1 (13¾-ounce) can
    COLLEGE INN® Beef
    Broth
2 tablespoons WRIGHT'S®
    Natural Hickory
    Seasoning
2 cups green or red bell
    pepper slices
2 cups onion wedges
3 ears corn-on-the-cob, cut
    into 1-inch chunks

In shallow bowl, combine flour, garlic salt and ground red pepper. Coat beef with flour mixture. In 8-quart saucepan, brown beef in oil. Add beef broth and hickory seasoning. Bring to a boil; reduce heat. Cover tightly and simmer 2 hours. Add peppers, onions and corn. Cover; simmer 45 minutes longer or until vegetables and beef are fork-tender. To serve, thinly slice beef and serve with vegetables and sauce. *Makes 6 servings*

Bistro Burgundy Stew

1 pound sirloin beef, cut
    into 1½-inch pieces
3 tablespoons all-purpose
    flour
6 slices bacon, cut into
    1-inch pieces (about
    ¼ pound)
2 cloves garlic, pressed
3 carrots, peeled and cut
    into 1-inch pieces (about
    1½ cups)
¾ cup Burgundy or other dry
    red wine
½ cup GREY POUPON®
    Dijon Mustard or
    GREY POUPON® Country
    Dijon Mustard
12 small mushrooms
1½ cups scallions, cut into
    1½-inch pieces

Coat beef with flour; set aside.
In large skillet, over medium heat,
cook bacon just until done; pour
off excess fat. Add beef and garlic;
cook until browned. Stir in
carrots, wine and mustard; cover.
Simmer 30 minutes or until carrots
are tender, stirring occasionally.
Stir in mushrooms and scallions;
cook 10 minutes more, stirring
occasionally. Garnish as desired.
Makes 6 servings

Santa Fe Burrito Bake

1½ pounds ground beef
1 cup water
1 can (4 ounces) chopped
    green chilies, undrained
1 package (1.25 ounces) taco
    seasoning mix, dry
2 cups Wheat CHEX® brand
    cereal, crushed to ¾ cup
1 loaf frozen bread dough,
    thawed
1 cup (4 ounces) shredded
    Cheddar cheese
1 teaspoon margarine or
    butter, melted
  Chili powder
  Salsa, sour cream and
    shredded lettuce

Preheat oven to 350°F. In large
skillet over medium heat cook
meat 5 minutes or until no longer
pink; drain. Stir in water, chilies
and seasoning mix. Add cereal,
stirring until well combined; set
aside. Roll bread dough into a
15x10-inch rectangle. Spread 2
cups reserved meat mixture in a
4-inch-wide strip lengthwise down
center of dough. Top with cheese.
Cover with remaining meat
mixture. Bring sides of dough up
over filling. Seal top and sides
well. Place seam side down on
ungreased baking sheet. Brush
with margarine. Sprinkle with chili
powder. Bake 30 to 35 minutes or
until golden brown. Slice and
serve with salsa, sour cream and
lettuce.   *Makes 6 servings*

To decorate top: Cut 1-inch wide
strip from a short side of dough;
reserve. Decorate loaf with
reserved dough before brushing
with margarine.

Santa Fe Burrito Bake

Tex-Mex Two Bean Chili

Roman Meal®
Company Meat Loaf

1 pound lean ground beef
1/2 cup ROMAN MEAL® Wheat, Rye, Bran, Flax or Oats, Wheat, Rye, Bran, Flax Cereal
1/2 cup milk or tomato juice
1/4 cup finely chopped onion
1/4 cup finely chopped celery
1 egg, slightly beaten
2 teaspoons Worcestershire Sauce
1/2 to 1 teaspoon salt or garlic salt
1/8 teaspoon pepper

Preheat oven to 350°F. In large bowl combine all ingredients; mix well. Shape into ring in 8-inch cake pan. If desired, spread with mixture of 2 tablespoons brown sugar, 2 tablespoons catsup and 1 teaspoon prepared mustard. Bake 40 to 50 minutes, or until browned; let stand 10 minutes.

Makes 6 servings

Tex-Mex
Two Bean Chili

2 tablespoons olive oil
1 cup chopped onions
1 cup chopped green pepper
2 large cloves garlic, pressed
1 pound lean stew meat, cut into 1/2-inch cubes
1/2 pound bulk hot Italian sausage*
1 3/4 cups (15-ounce can) CONTADINA® Tomato Puree
1 3/4 cups (14 1/2-ounce can) beef broth
1 1/4 cups water
2/3 cup (6-ounce can) CONTADINA® Tomato Paste
1/2 cup (4-ounce can) diced green chiles
3 tablespoons chili powder
1 1/2 teaspoons ground cumin
1 teaspoon salt
1 teaspoon sugar
1 teaspoon dried oregano leaves, crushed
1/8 teaspoon cayenne pepper (optional)
1 1/2 cups (15-ounce can) pinto beans, rinsed and drained
1 1/2 cups (15-ounce can) kidney beans, rinsed and drained

*Note: If link sausage is used, remove casings before sautéing.

In 6-quart saucepan, heat oil; sauté onion, green pepper and garlic 3 to 4 minutes, or until tender. Add stew meat and sausage, stirring to crumble sausage; cook 5 to 6 minutes. Blend in tomato puree, broth, water, tomato paste, green chiles, chili powder, cumin, salt, sugar, oregano and cayenne pepper. Bring to a boil. Reduce heat; simmer uncovered 1½ hours, stirring occasionally. Mix in beans. Cover and simmer additional 30 minutes.   *Makes 6 servings*

Patchwork Casserole

- **2 pounds ground beef**
- **2 cups chopped green bell pepper**
- **1 cup chopped onion**
- **2 pounds frozen Southern-style hash-brown potatoes, thawed**
- **2 cans (8 ounces each) tomato sauce**
- **1 cup water**
- **1 can (6 ounces) tomato paste**
- **1 teaspoon salt**
- **½ teaspoon dried basil, crumbled**
- **¼ teaspoon ground black pepper**
- **1 pound pasteurized process American cheese, thinly sliced**

Cook and stir beef in large skillet over medium heat until crumbled and brown, about 10 minutes; drain off fat.

Add green pepper and onion; sauté until tender, about 4 minutes. Stir in all remaining ingredients except cheese.

Spoon ½ of the meat mixture into 13 × 9 × 2-inch baking pan or 3-quart baking dish; top with ½ of the cheese. Spoon remaining meat mixture evenly on top of cheese.

Cover pan with aluminum foil. Bake in preheated 350°F oven 45 minutes.

Cut remaining cheese into decorative shapes; place on top of casserole. Let stand, loosely covered, until cheese melts, about 5 minutes.

Makes 8 to 10 servings

Patchwork Casserole

Santa Fe Stew Olé

1 tablespoon vegetable oil
1½ pounds beef stew meat, cut
    into small bite-size
    pieces
1 can (28 ounces) stewed
    tomatoes, undrained
2 medium carrots, sliced
    into ¼-inch pieces
1 medium onion, coarsely
    chopped
1 package (1.25 ounces)
    LAWRY'S® Taco Spices &
    Seasonings
2 tablespoons diced green
    chiles
½ teaspoon LAWRY'S®
    Seasoned Salt
¼ cup water
2 tablespoons all-purpose
    flour
1 can (15 ounces) pinto
    beans, drained

In Dutch oven, heat oil; brown
stew meat. Add tomatoes, carrots,
onion, Taco Spices & Seasonings,
green chiles and Seasoned Salt;
blend well. Bring to a boil; reduce
heat. Cover and simmer 40
minutes. In small bowl, combine
water and flour; blend well. Add
to stew mixture. Stir in pinto
beans and simmer an additional 15
minutes.   *Makes 4 servings*

Presentation: Serve hearty
portions of stew with cornbread
or warm tortillas.

Cottage Meat Loaf

1 pound ground beef
1 cup cottage cheese
⅓ cup fresh bread crumbs
1 egg, beaten
1 medium onion, finely
    chopped
¼ cup chopped green pepper
2 teaspoons paprika
½ teaspoon salt
¼ teaspoon pepper
⅛ teaspoon nutmeg
¼ cup chili sauce (optional)

Combine all ingredients except
chili sauce in large bowl; mix
well. Place in loaf pan or shape
into round in pie plate. Pour chili
sauce over top, if desired. Bake in
preheated 350°F oven about 45
minutes or until no longer pink in
center.   *Makes 4 to 6 servings*

Favorite recipe from **Wisconsin Milk
Marketing Board** © 1992

Santa Fe Stew Olé

Mexican Beef Stir-Fry

1 pound beef flank steak
2 tablespoons vegetable oil
1 teaspoon ground cumin
1 teaspoon garlic salt
1 teaspoon dried oregano
    leaves
1 red bell pepper, cut into
    thin strips
1 medium onion, chopped
1 to 2 jalapeño peppers,
    seeded and cut into
    slivers*

Cut beef flank steak diagonally across the grain into 1/8-inch-thick slices. Combine oil, cumin, garlic salt and oregano. Heat 1 tablespoon of the oil mixture in large nonstick frying pan until hot. Add red pepper, onion and jalapeño pepper; stir-fry over medium-high heat 2 to 3 minutes or until tender-crisp. Remove from pan; reserve. Stir-fry beef strips (1/2 at a time) in remaining oil mixture 1 to 2 minutes. Return vegetables to frying pan and heat through.

Makes 4 servings

Serving Suggestions: Mexican Beef Stir-Fry may be served on a lettuce raft, in taco shells or on tostada shells. Top with guacamole, if desired.

Preparation time: 15 minutes
Cooking time: 10 minutes

Favorite recipe from **National Live Stock and Meat Board**

*Wear rubber gloves when working with jalapeño peppers and wash hands with warm soapy water. Avoid touching face or eyes.

18-Minute Meatball Soup

1 pound ground beef (80%
    lean)
1 can (16 ounces) stewed
    tomatoes, broken up
1 can (13 3/4 ounces) beef
    broth
1/2 cup salsa or picante sauce
3/4 teaspoon ground coriander
3/4 teaspoon ground cumin
1/2 teaspoon salt
2 medium zucchini, thinly
    sliced
2 1/2 tablespoons chopped
    cilantro

Combine tomatoes, beef broth and salsa in 2 1/2-quart microwave-safe casserole. Cover and microwave at HIGH (100% power) 6 minutes. Meanwhile combine ground beef, coriander, cumin and salt; mix lightly but thoroughly. Pinch off 1-inch pieces of beef mixture to make approximately 32 free-form meatballs; place around the sides of 8-inch microwave-safe baking dish. Remove tomato mixture from microwave; add zucchini, cover and reserve. Cover meatballs with waxed paper and cook at HIGH 2 1/2 minutes, rotating dish 1/4 turn after 1 1/2 minutes. Remove meatballs with slotted spoon and place in tomato mixture. Cook tomato mixture with meatballs, covered, at HIGH 4 1/2 minutes. Garnish with cilantro.

Makes 4 servings

Preparation time: 5 minutes
Cooking time: 13 minutes

Favorite recipe from **National Live Stock and Meat Board**

Mexican Beef Stir-Fry

Santa Fe Casserole Bake

1 pound lean ground beef
1 package (1.25 ounces) LAWRY'S® Taco Spices & Seasonings
2 cups chicken broth
¼ cup all-purpose flour
1 cup dairy sour cream
1 can (7 ounces) diced green chiles
1 package (11 ounces) corn or tortilla chips
2 cups (8 ounces) grated Monterey Jack or Cheddar cheese
½ cup sliced green onions with tops

Santa Fe Casserole Bake

In medium skillet, brown meat and stir until crumbly; drain fat. Add Taco Spices & Seasonings; blend well. In small bowl, combine broth and flour. Add to meat mixture, bring to a boil to slightly thicken liquid. Stir in sour cream and chiles; blend well. In 13×9×2-inch lightly greased glass baking dish, place ½ of chips. Top with ½ of beef mixture, ½ of sauce, ½ of cheese and ½ of green onions. Layer again with remaining ingredients ending with green onions. Bake, uncovered, in 375°F oven for 20 minutes. Let stand 5 minutes before serving.

Microwave Directions: In 1-quart glass bowl, crumble beef. Microwave on HIGH 5 to 6 minutes, stirring once; drain fat. Add Taco Spices & Seasonings; blend well and set aside. In 1-quart glass measuring cup, combine broth and flour. Microwave on HIGH 5 minutes or until bubbling and thick, stirring once. Add to meat mixture; stir well. Stir in sour cream and chiles. In a 13×9×2-inch lightly greased microwave-safe baking dish, layer as stated above. Cover with waxed paper. Microwave on 50% power 15 to 18 minutes, rotating after 7 minutes. Let stand 5 minutes before serving.

Makes 6 servings

Presentation: Serve with gazpacho salad and Mexican-style rice.

Hint: Top with guacamole for additional flavor.

Stir-Fried Beef and Vegetables

1 (³/₄- to 1-pound) flank
   steak, cut diagonally into
   ¹/₈-inch diagonal slices
1 large sweet onion, sliced
8 ounces fresh mushrooms,
   sliced (about 2 cups)
1 green bell pepper, seeded
   and cut into strips
1 clove garlic, finely
   chopped
2 teaspoons WYLER'S® or
   STEERO® Beef-Flavor
   Instant Bouillon *or*
   2 Beef-Flavor Bouillon
   Cubes
¹/₃ cup boiling water
¹/₄ cup soy sauce
2 tablespoons cider vinegar
2¹/₂ teaspoons cornstarch
1 teaspoon sugar
¹/₄ cup vegetable oil
1 (8-ounce) can sliced water
   chestnuts, drained

Prepare meat and vegetables.
Dissolve bouillon in water.
Combine soy sauce, vinegar,
cornstarch and sugar; stir into
bouillon mixture. In large heavy
skillet or wok, heat *2 tablespoons*
oil over high heat. Add garlic and
meat; stir-fry 2 minutes (meat will
be slightly pink in center). Remove
meat and juices. Wipe pan; heat
1 tablespoon oil. Add onion,
mushrooms, green pepper and
water chestnuts; stir-fry 2 minutes
over high heat. Add remaining
1 tablespoon oil around edge of
pan; add meat and juices, then
bouillon mixture. Stir; cover and
cook 2 minutes. Refrigerate
leftovers.   *Makes 4 servings*

Stir-Fried Beef and Vegetables

Beef Barley Vegetable Soup

1 pound beef shanks,
   cracked
7 cups water
1 (14¹/₄-ounce) can stewed
   tomatoes
³/₄ cup chopped onion
2 tablespoons WYLER'S® or
   STEERO® Beef-Flavor
   Instant Bouillon *or*
   6 Beef-Flavor Bouillon
   Cubes
¹/₂ teaspoon basil leaves
1 bay leaf
¹/₂ cup uncooked regular
   barley
3 medium carrots, peeled
   and chopped
1¹/₂ cups chopped celery

In large kettle or Dutch oven,
combine shanks, water, tomatoes,
onion, bouillon, basil and bay leaf.
Bring to a boil. Reduce heat; cover
and simmer 1 hour. Remove
shanks from stock; cut meat into
¹/₂-inch pieces. Skim off fat. Add
meat and barley; bring to a boil.
Reduce heat; cover and simmer 30
minutes. Add carrots and celery;
cook 30 minutes longer. Remove
bay leaf. Refrigerate leftovers.
         Makes about 10 servings

Cheeseburger Pie

1 (9-inch) unbaked pastry
　　shell, pricked
8 slices BORDEN® Process
　　American Cheese Food
1 pound lean ground beef
½ cup tomato sauce
⅓ cup chopped green bell
　　pepper
⅓ cup chopped onion
1 teaspoon WYLER'S® or
　　STEERO® Beef-Flavor
　　Instant Bouillon *or*
　　1 Beef-Flavor Bouillon
　　Cube
3 eggs, well beaten
2 tablespoons flour

Preheat oven to 450°F. Bake
pastry shell 8 minutes; remove
from oven. *Reduce oven
temperature to 350°F.* Cut *6 slices*
cheese food into pieces. In large
skillet, brown meat; pour off fat.
Add tomato sauce, green pepper,
onion and bouillon; cook and stir
until bouillon dissolves. Remove
from heat; stir in eggs, flour and
cheese food pieces. Turn into
prepared pastry shell. Bake 20 to
25 minutes or until hot. Arrange
remaining *2 slices* cheese food on
top. Bake 3 to 5 minutes longer or
until cheese food begins to melt.
Refrigerate leftovers.

Makes one 9-inch pie

Beef Pot Roast in Beer

3- to 4-pound beef rump
　　roast
2 tablespoons flour
1 teaspoon salt
　　Dash pepper
2 tablespoons CRISCO®
　　Shortening
1 can (12 ounces) beer
2 bay leaves
6 small whole onions, peeled
4 medium carrots, peeled
　　and cut into 1-inch
　　pieces
½ cup cold water
¼ cup flour
2 tablespoons catsup

Coat roast with 2 tablespoons
flour. Season with salt and pepper.
In Dutch oven or large skillet,
brown roast on all sides in hot
Crisco®. Add ½ cup of the beer
and the bay leaves. Cover tightly;
simmer 1½ hours. Remove bay
leaves. Add onions and carrots.
Cover and cook 1 hour more or
until meat and vegetables are
tender; remove to heated platter.
Skim fat from pan juices. Add
enough of the remaining beer to
make 1½ cups liquid. Combine
cold water and ¼ cup flour; stir
into juices with catsup. Cook and
stir until thickened and bubbly.
Cook and stir 2 to 3 minutes more.
Serve with meat and vegetables.

Makes 6 to 8 servings

Cheeseburger Pie

PLEASING
POULTRY

Forty-Clove Chicken Filice

1 (3-pound) frying chicken, cut into serving pieces
40 cloves fresh garlic, peeled and left whole
½ cup dry white wine
¼ cup dry vermouth
¼ cup olive oil
4 ribs celery, thickly sliced
2 tablespoons finely chopped parsley
2 teaspoons dried basil
1 teaspoon dried oregano
Pinch of crushed red pepper
1 lemon
Salt and black pepper to taste

Preheat oven to 375°F. Place chicken pieces, skin-side up, in a single layer in shallow baking pan. Combine garlic, wine, vermouth, oil, celery, parsley, basil, oregano and red pepper in medium-sized bowl; mix thoroughly. Pour garlic mixture over chicken pieces. Remove peel from lemon in thin strips; place peel throughout pan. Squeeze juice from lemon and sprinkle over the top. Season with salt and black pepper. Cover pan with aluminum foil. Bake 40 minutes. Remove foil and bake another 15 minutes. Garnish as desired.

Makes 4 to 6 servings

Favorite recipe from **The Fresh Garlic Association**

Forty-Clove Chicken Filice

Chicken and Rice Paprikash

3 teaspoons paprika, divided
¾ teaspoon salt
¼ teaspoon pepper
6 medium chicken thighs
1 can (14½ or 16 ounces) whole tomatoes
1 small onion, sliced and separated into rings
1 teaspoon chicken bouillon granules
2 cloves garlic, minced
1 cup UNCLE BEN'S® CONVERTED® Brand Rice, uncooked
1 large green pepper, cut into thin strips
Light sour cream or plain yogurt (optional)

Combine 1½ teaspoons of the paprika, salt and pepper. Rub seasonings onto chicken thighs, coating all surfaces with mixture; set aside. Drain tomatoes, reserving juice. Chop tomatoes; set aside. Add enough water to juice to equal 2 cups. Combine tomato liquid, onion, bouillon granules, garlic and remaining 1½ teaspoons paprika in 12-inch skillet. Bring to a boil. Stir in rice and chopped tomatoes. Arrange chicken thighs on top of rice mixture. Cover tightly and simmer 20 minutes. Add green pepper. Remove from heat. Let stand covered until all liquid is absorbed, about 5 minutes. Serve with light sour cream or plain yogurt, if desired.

Makes 6 servings

Turkey 'n Stuffing Bake

½ cup (1 stick) butter or margarine
1¼ cups boiling water
3½ cups seasoned stuffing crumbs*
1 can (2.8 ounces) DURKEE® French Fried Onions
1 can (10¾ ounces) condensed cream of celery soup
¾ cup milk
1½ cups (7 ounces) cubed, cooked turkey
1 package (10 ounces) frozen peas, thawed

Combine butter and water; stir until butter melts. Pour over seasoned stuffing crumbs; toss lightly. Stir in *½ can* Durkee® French Fried Onions. Spoon stuffing mixture into 9-inch shallow baking dish. Press stuffing across bottom and up sides of dish to form a shell. Combine soup, milk, turkey and peas; pour into stuffing shell. Bake, covered, at 350°F for 30 minutes. Top with remaining onions and bake, uncovered, 5 minutes longer.

Makes 4 to 6 servings

*Three cups leftover stuffing may be substituted for butter, water, and stuffing crumbs. If stuffing is dry, stir in water, 1 tablespoon at a time, until moist but not wet.

Hearty Turkey Chili

Hearty Turkey Chili

1 cup chopped onions
1 cup chopped green pepper
2 cloves garlic, minced
1 tablespoon vegetable oil
2 pounds ground raw turkey
2 cans (14½ ounces each)
    tomatoes, cut into bite-
    size pieces
1 bottle (12 ounces) HEINZ®
    Chili Sauce
1 tablespoon chili powder
1 teaspoon lemon pepper
    seasoning
1 teaspoon dried basil
    leaves, crushed
½ teaspoon dried thyme
    leaves, crushed
⅛ to ¼ teaspoon hot
    pepper sauce
2 cans (15½ ounces each)
    kidney beans, drained
    Sliced green onions
    Shredded Cheddar cheese
    Dairy sour cream or plain
    yogurt

In Dutch oven, sauté onions, green pepper and garlic in oil until tender. Add turkey and cook until lightly browned. Add tomatoes, chili sauce, chili powder, lemon pepper, basil, thyme and hot pepper sauce. Cover; simmer 45 minutes. Add kidney beans; simmer, covered, an additional 20 minutes. Serve topped with green onions, cheese and sour cream.

Makes 8 servings

Baked Chicken Reuben

4 whole chicken breasts,
   split, skinned and boned
1/4 teaspoon salt
1/8 teaspoon pepper
1 can (16 ounces) sauerkraut,
   well drained
4 (6×4-inch) slices Swiss
   cheese
1¼ cups Thousand Island
   salad dressing

Preheat oven to 325°F. Place chicken in single layer in greased baking pan. Sprinkle with salt and pepper. Press excess liquid from sauerkraut; spoon over chicken. Arrange cheese slices over sauerkraut. Pour dressing evenly over the top. Cover pan with aluminum foil. Bake about 1½ hours or until chicken is tender.

Makes 6 to 8 servings

Favorite recipe from **National Broiler Council**

Ranch-Style Chicken Casserole

1 envelope LIPTON® Onion
   Recipe Soup Mix
1½ cups buttermilk
1 tablespoon all-purpose
   flour
2 cloves garlic, finely
   chopped
4 boneless skinless chicken
   breast halves
2 cups frozen mixed
   vegetables
1/4 cup dry bread crumbs
1 tablespoon butter or
   margarine, melted
   Paprika (optional)

Preheat oven to 350°F.

In small bowl, thoroughly combine onion recipe soup mix, buttermilk, flour and garlic; set aside.

In lightly greased 2-quart shallow casserole, arrange chicken breasts and vegetables; add soup mixture. Bake, covered, 20 minutes.

Remove cover and top with bread crumbs combined with butter. Continue baking, uncovered, 25 minutes. Sprinkle, if desired, with paprika.   *Makes 4 servings*

Baked Chicken Reuben

Chicken Parisian

Chicken Parisian

¹/₄ cup unsifted flour
¹/₄ teaspoon paprika
¹/₄ teaspoon pepper
6 skinless boneless chicken
breast halves (about
1¹/₂ pounds)
3 tablespoons margarine or
butter
8 ounces fresh mushrooms,
sliced (about 2 cups)
¹/₂ cup water
¹/₄ cup dry white wine
2 teaspoons WYLER'S® or
STEERO® Chicken-Flavor
Instant Bouillon or 2
Chicken-Flavor Bouillon
Cubes
2 teaspoons chopped parsley
¹/₄ teaspoon dried thyme
leaves

In plastic bag, combine flour, paprika and pepper. Add chicken, a few pieces at a time; shake to coat. In skillet, brown chicken in margarine; remove from pan. In same skillet, add remaining ingredients; simmer 3 minutes. Add chicken; simmer covered 20 minutes or until tender. Refrigerate leftovers. *Makes 6 servings*

Sweet & Sour Meatballs with Vegetables

1 pound ground turkey
2 cups Multi-Bran CHEX®
brand cereal, crushed to
³/₄ cup
¹/₄ cup chopped onion
1 egg, beaten or ¹/₄ cup
cholesterol-free egg
product
2 tablespoons chopped fresh
parsley
1 clove garlic, minced
1 teaspoon lite soy sauce
¹/₄ teaspoon ground ginger
¹/₄ cup water
16 ounces frozen Oriental or
mixed vegetables,
prepared according to
package directions,
drained
1 cup prepared sweet and
sour sauce
Hot cooked rice (optional)

In medium bowl combine turkey, cereal, onion, egg, parsley, garlic, soy sauce and ginger. Mix well. Using 1 rounded tablespoon meat mixture for each, shape into 2-inch balls. Brown meatballs in lightly greased skillet over medium heat, turning often. Add water; cover and cook over low heat 8 to 10 minutes or until no longer pink, stirring occasionally. Drain. Add vegetables and sweet and sour sauce; cook over low heat, stirring gently until meatballs are coated and sauce and vegetables are warm. Serve over rice, if desired.
Makes 6 servings

Chicken Costa Brava Casserole

1 can (20 oz.) DOLE®
    Pineapple Slices in Juice
6 boneless skinless chicken
    breast halves, cut in half
Salt and pepper
¼ cup flour
1 teaspoon cinnamon
1 teaspoon cumin
1 teaspoon dried oregano
3 tablespoons olive oil
2 cloves garlic, pressed
1 large onion, cut in wedges
2 jars (12 oz. each) salsa
1 can (8 oz.) stewed tomatoes
1 cup pitted black olives
1 cup pimento-stuffed olives
2 teaspoons cornstarch
2 tablespoons water
1 DOLE® Red Bell Pepper,
    slivered

Drain pineapple; reserve juice. Sprinkle chicken with salt and pepper. Combine flour, cinnamon, cumin and oregano. Coat chicken with flour mixture. In ovenproof skillet, sauté chicken in oil until browned. Add garlic and onion; cook until onion is soft. Add reserved juice, salsa, tomatoes and olives. Stir to blend. Bake in skillet, covered, in 400°F oven 30 minutes. Mix cornstarch with water. Stir into pan juices; add bell pepper. Cook over medium heat 10 minutes longer until sauce boils and thickens. Add pineapple; spoon sauce over.   *Makes 12 servings*

Preparation time: 10 minutes
Cooking time: 45 minutes

Turkey Vegetable Roll-Ups

½ cup *each* thin strips
    carrots, red bell pepper,
    summer squash and
    zucchini
4 (4-ounce) fresh turkey
    breast slices
¼ cup unsifted flour
¼ teaspoon paprika
2 tablespoons vegetable oil
⅓ cup water
¼ cup REALEMON® Lemon
    Juice from Concentrate
2 tablespoons dry sherry,
    optional
1 teaspoon WYLER'S® or
    STEERO® Chicken-Flavor
    Instant Bouillon
½ teaspoon thyme leaves
    Hot cooked pasta or rice

Place equal amounts of vegetables on center of turkey slices; roll up from narrow edge. Combine flour and paprika; coat roll-ups. In large skillet, brown roll-ups in oil. Add remaining ingredients; cover and simmer 10 minutes or until turkey is no longer pink. Serve with hot cooked pasta or rice. Refrigerate leftovers.   *Makes 4 servings*

Turkey Vegetable Roll-Ups

Dairyland Confetti Chicken

CASSEROLE
1 cup diced carrots
3/4 cup chopped onion
1/2 cup diced celery
1/4 cup chicken broth
1 can (10 1/2 ounces) cream of chicken soup
1 cup dairy sour cream
3 cups cubed cooked chicken
1/2 cup (4 ounces) sliced mushrooms
1 teaspoon Worcestershire sauce
1 teaspoon salt
1/8 teaspoon pepper

CONFETTI TOPPING
1 cup sifted all-purpose flour
2 teaspoons baking powder
1/2 teaspoon salt
2 eggs, slightly beaten
1/2 cup milk
1 tablespoon chopped green bell pepper
1 tablespoon chopped pimiento
1 1/4 cups (5 ounces) shredded Wisconsin Cheddar cheese, divided

For casserole: In saucepan, combine carrots, onion, celery and chicken broth. Simmer 20 minutes. In 3-quart casserole, mix soup, sour cream, chicken cubes, mushrooms, Worcestershire sauce, salt and pepper. Add simmered vegetables and liquid; mix well.

For confetti topping: In mixing bowl, combine flour, baking powder and salt. Add eggs, milk, green pepper, pimiento and 1 cup of the cheese. Mix just until well blended. Drop tablespoons of topping onto casserole and bake in 350°F oven for 40 to 45 minutes or until golden brown. Sprinkle with remaining 1/4 cup cheese and return to oven until melted. Garnish as desired.
Makes 6 to 8 servings

Favorite recipe from **Wisconsin Milk Marketing Board** ©1992

Chicken Noodle Soup

1 (46-fluid ounce) can COLLEGE INN® Chicken Broth
1/2 pound skinless boneless chicken, cut into bite-size pieces
1 1/2 cups uncooked medium egg noodles
1 cup sliced carrots
1/2 cup chopped onion
1/3 cup sliced celery
1 teaspoon dried dill weed
1/4 teaspoon ground black pepper

In large saucepan, over medium-high heat, bring chicken broth, chicken, noodles, carrots, onion, celery, dill and pepper to a boil. Reduce heat; simmer 20 minutes or until chicken and noodles are cooked.   *Makes 8 servings*

Dairyland Confetti Chicken

Kung Pao Chicken

Kung Pao Chicken

5 teaspoons soy sauce,
    divided
5 teaspoons dry sherry,
    divided
3 1/2 teaspoons cornstarch,
    divided
1/4 teaspoon salt
3 skinless boneless chicken
    breast halves, cut into
    bite-size pieces
2 tablespoons chicken broth
    or water
1 tablespoon red wine
    vinegar
1 1/2 teaspoons sugar
3 tablespoons vegetable oil,
    divided
1/3 cup salted peanuts
6 to 8 small dried hot chili
    peppers
1 1/2 teaspoons minced fresh
    ginger
2 green onions, cut into
    1 1/2-inch pieces

For marinade, combine 2 teaspoons of the soy sauce, 2 teaspoons sherry, 2 teaspoons cornstarch and the salt in large bowl; mix well. Add chicken; stir to coat well. Let stand 30 minutes. Combine remaining 3 teaspoons soy sauce, 3 teaspoons sherry, chicken broth, vinegar, sugar and remaining 1 1/2 teaspoons cornstarch in small bowl; mix well and set aside. Heat 1 tablespoon of the oil in wok or large skillet over medium heat. Add peanuts and cook until golden. Remove peanuts and set aside. Heat remaining 2 tablespoons oil in wok over medium heat. Add chili peppers and stir-fry until peppers just begin to darken, about 1 minute. Increase heat to high. Add chicken and stir-fry 2 minutes. Add ginger; stir-fry until chicken is cooked through, about 1 minute more. Add onions and peanuts to wok. Stir chicken broth mixture and add to pan; cook and stir until sauce boils and thickens.

Makes 3 servings

Cheesy Chicken Tetrazzini

2 whole skinless boneless chicken breasts, cut into 1-inch pieces (about 1½ pounds)
2 tablespoons butter or margarine
1½ cups sliced mushrooms
1 small red pepper, cut into julienne strips
½ cup sliced green onions
¼ cup all-purpose flour
1¾ cups chicken broth
1 cup light cream or half-and-half
2 tablespoons dry sherry
½ teaspoon salt
¼ teaspoon black pepper
¼ teaspoon dried thyme, crushed
1 package (8 ounces) tri-color rotelle pasta, cooked until just tender and drained
¼ cup grated Parmesan cheese
2 tablespoons chopped parsley
1 cup shredded NOKKELOST® (or Jarlsberg) cheese

In skillet, brown chicken in butter. Add mushrooms; cook until brown. Add red pepper and green onions; cook several minutes, stirring occasionally. Stir in flour and cook several minutes until blended. Gradually blend in chicken broth, cream and sherry. Cook, stirring, until thickened and smooth. Add salt, black pepper and thyme. Toss with pasta, Parmesan cheese and parsley. Spoon into 1½-quart lightly greased baking dish. Bake at 350°F 30 minutes. Top with cheese. Bake until cheese is melted.

Makes 6 servings

Green Chile Chicken

1 pound skinless boneless chicken breasts, cut into thin strips
1 medium onion, sliced
1 clove garlic, pressed
2 tablespoons vegetable oil
1 (12-ounce) jar ORTEGA® Mild Thick and Chunky Salsa
1 (4-ounce) can ORTEGA® Diced Green Chiles
½ teaspoon dried oregano leaves
Hot cooked rice or flour tortillas
Dairy sour cream, optional

In medium skillet, over medium-high heat, cook chicken, onion and garlic in oil until chicken is no longer pink. Add salsa, chiles and oregano. Simmer, uncovered, 10 minutes. Serve over rice or in tortillas. Top with sour cream, if desired. *Makes 4 to 6 servings*

Fancy Chicken Puff Pie

¼ cup butter or margarine
¼ cup chopped shallots
¼ cup all-purpose flour
1 cup chicken stock or broth
¼ cup sherry
 Salt to taste
⅛ teaspoon white pepper
 Pinch ground nutmeg
¼ pound ham, cut into
  2 × ¼-inch strips
3 cups cooked **PERDUE®**
  chicken, cut into
  2 × ¼-inch strips
1½ cups fresh asparagus
  pieces *or* 1 (10-ounce)
  package frozen
  asparagus pieces
1 cup (½ pint) heavy cream
 Chilled pie crust for a
  1-crust pie *or* 1 sheet
  frozen puff pastry
1 egg, beaten

In medium saucepan, over medium-high heat, melt butter; sauté shallots lightly. Stir in flour; cook 3 minutes. Add broth and sherry. Heat to boiling, stirring constantly; season to taste with salt, pepper and nutmeg. Reduce heat to low and simmer 5 minutes. Stir in ham, chicken, asparagus and cream. Pour chicken mixture into ungreased 9-inch pie plate.

Preheat oven to 425°F. Cut 8-inch circle from crust. Cut hearts from extra dough with cookie cutter, if desired. Place circle on cookie sheet moistened with cold water. Pierce with fork, brush with egg and decorate with hearts; brush hearts with egg.

Bake crust and filled pie plate 10 minutes; *reduce heat to 350°F* and bake additional 10 to 15 minutes or until pastry is golden brown and filling is hot and set. With a spatula, place pastry over hot filling and serve immediately.

Makes 4 servings

Fancy Chicken Puff Pie

Quick Chicken Cacciatore

4 (4-ounce) boneless chicken
   breast halves, lightly
   seasoned with salt and
   pepper
  Flour
2 cloves garlic, finely
   chopped
4 tablespoons olive oil,
   divided
1 (26-ounce) jar CLASSICO®
   Di Napoli (Tomato &
   Basil) or Di Sicilia (Ripe
   Olives & Mushrooms)
   Pasta Sauce
1 small green bell pepper,
   cut into strips
1 small red bell pepper, cut
   into strips
2 slices Provolone cheese,
   cut in half
1 (7-ounce) package or 2
   cups CREAMETTES®
   Elbow Macaroni, cooked
   as package directs and
   drained
  Chopped parsley

Coat chicken with flour. In large
skillet, brown chicken and garlic
in *3 tablespoons* oil; remove
chicken from pan. Add pasta sauce
then chicken. Bring to a boil;
reduce heat. Cover and simmer 20
minutes, adding peppers during
last 5 minutes. Uncover; top each
chicken breast with half cheese
slice. Toss hot cooked macaroni
with remaining *1 tablespoon* oil
and parsley. Serve with chicken
and sauce. Refrigerate leftovers.

Makes 4 servings

Quick Chicken Cacciatore

Turkey and Wild Rice Bake

1 package (6 ounces) wild
   and white rice mix,
   uncooked
2 1/3 cups water
2 cups cooked turkey, cubed
1 can (4 ounces) mushrooms,
   drained
1 can (14 ounces) whole
   artichoke hearts, drained
   and quartered
1 jar (2 ounces) chopped
   pimiento, drained
1 cup shredded Swiss cheese

Preheat oven to 350°F. In 2-quart
lightly greased casserole combine
rice with seasoning packet, water,
turkey, mushrooms, artichokes and
pimiento. Cover and bake 1 hour
and 15 minutes or until liquid is
absorbed.

Top casserole with cheese. Return
to oven and bake, uncovered, 5 to
10 minutes or until cheese is
melted and golden brown.

Makes 6 servings

Favorite recipe from **National Turkey
Federation**

Turkey a la King

⅓ cup **BUTTER FLAVOR CRISCO®**
⅓ cup chopped green pepper
2 tablespoons chopped green onion
5 tablespoons all-purpose flour
1 teaspoon seasoned salt
⅛ teaspoon pepper
1½ cups milk
¾ cup water
1 teaspoon instant chicken bouillon granules
2 cups cubed cooked turkey or chicken
1 can (8 ounces) mushroom stems and pieces, drained
1 cup frozen peas
1 jar (2 ounces) sliced pimiento, drained
   Toast points or patty shells
¼ cup sliced or slivered almonds, optional

In 3-quart saucepan melt Butter Flavor Crisco®. Add green pepper and onion. Cook and stir over medium heat until tender. Stir in flour, seasoned salt and pepper. Blend in milk, water and bouillon granules. Cook and stir over medium heat for about 10 minutes, or until mixture thickens and bubbles. Stir in turkey, mushrooms, peas and pimiento. Continue cooking for about 5 minutes, or until hot and peas are tender. Serve over toast points or in patty shells. Top with almonds, if desired.   *Makes 4 to 6 servings*

Apple Curry Chicken

2 whole chicken breasts, split, skinned and boned
1 cup apple juice, divided
¼ teaspoon salt
   Dash of pepper
1½ cups plain croutons
1 medium-size apple, chopped
½ cup finely chopped onion
¼ cup raisins
2 teaspoons brown sugar
1 teaspoon curry powder
¾ teaspoon poultry seasoning
⅛ teaspoon garlic powder

Preheat oven to 350°F. Lightly grease shallow baking dish. Arrange chicken breasts in a single layer in prepared pan. Combine ¼ cup of the apple juice, the salt and pepper in small bowl. Brush all of mixture over chicken. Combine croutons, apple, onion, raisins, sugar, curry powder, poultry seasoning and garlic powder in large bowl. Stir in remaining ¾ cup apple juice; spread over chicken. Cover; bake about 45 minutes or until chicken is tender. Garnish as desired.
Makes 4 servings

Favorite recipe from **Delmarva Poultry Industry, Inc.**

Apple Curry Chicken

Southwestern Chicken Soup

¼ pound bacon, diced
4 skinless boneless chicken
    breast halves, cut into
    cubes (about 1½ pounds)
3 cans (13¾ ounces each)
    chicken broth
2 teaspoons DURKEE® Garlic
    Powder
2 teaspoons DURKEE® Onion
    Powder
2 teaspoons DURKEE®
    Ground Cumin
1 teaspoon DURKEE® Thyme
    Leaves
4 cups assorted vegetables
    (such as celery, carrots,
    zucchini and red pepper)
    cut into bite-size pieces
1 package (10 ounces) frozen
    whole kernel corn,
    thawed
1 can (4 ounces) chopped
    mild green chilies,
    drained
    Shredded cheese, olives
    and tortilla chips
    (optional)

In Dutch oven or large saucepan
over medium-high heat, cook
bacon and chicken until chicken is
golden brown, about 5 minutes.
Add broth and seasonings. Bring to
a boil. Simmer, covered, 5 minutes.
Add vegetables and chilies; simmer,
covered, 5 minutes until vegetables
are tender. If desired, serve with
shredded cheese, olives and
tortilla chips.

Makes 6 servings

Southwestern Chicken Soup

Enchilada Casserole

1 can (20 oz.) DOLE®
    Pineapple Chunks in
    Syrup
2 cups diced cooked chicken
2 cups cottage cheese
¼ cup diced green chilies
¼ cup diced DOLE® Green
    Onion
½ teaspoon ground cumin
2 cans (10 oz. each)
    enchilada sauce
8 corn tortillas
1½ cups shredded Cheddar
    cheese
    Sour cream

Drain pineapple, reserve ¼ cup
syrup. Combine chicken, cottage
cheese, chilies, green onion and
cumin. Warm enchilada sauce
with pineapple and reserved
syrup. Dip tortillas in sauce.
Spoon chicken mixture in centers.
Roll; place seam-side down in
3-quart shallow casserole dish.
Top with remaining enchilada
sauce. Bake, covered, in 350°F
oven 20 to 25 minutes. Sprinkle
with cheese. Bake until cheese
melts. Let stand 10 minutes. Serve
with sour cream.

Makes 4 servings

Chicken Cashew

1 pound skinless boneless
    chicken breasts, cut into
    bite-size pieces
8 ounces fresh mushrooms,
    sliced (about 2 cups)
1/2 cup sliced green onions
1 green bell pepper, cut into
    strips
2 teaspoons WYLER'S® or
    STEERO® Chicken-Flavor
    Instant Bouillon *or*
    2 Chicken-Flavor
    Bouillon Cubes
1 1/4 cups boiling water
2 tablespoons soy sauce
1 tablespoon cornstarch
2 teaspoons light brown
    sugar
1/2 teaspoon ground ginger
2 tablespoons vegetable oil
1 (8-ounce) can sliced water
    chestnuts, drained
1/2 cup cashew nuts, divided
    Hot cooked rice

Prepare chicken and vegetables.
Dissolve bouillon in boiling water.
Combine soy sauce, cornstarch,
sugar and ginger; stir into bouillon
mixture. In large skillet or wok,
brown chicken in oil. Add
bouillon mixture; cook and stir
until slightly thickened. Add
mushrooms, green onions, green
pepper and water chestnuts;
simmer uncovered 5 to 8 minutes,
stirring occasionally. Remove from
heat; add *1/4 cup* nuts. Serve over
rice. Garnish with remaining nuts.
Refrigerate leftovers.

Makes 4 servings

Bird of Paradise

1 can (20 oz.) DOLE®
    Pineapple Slices in Syrup
4 chicken breast halves or
    3-pound fryer chicken,
    cut up
2 tablespoons margarine
1/4 cup dry sherry
3 tablespoons soy sauce
2 large cloves garlic, pressed
2 tablespoons minced
    crystallized ginger
1/2 teaspoon salt
1 DOLE® Red Bell Pepper,
    seeded, chunked
1 1/2 cups sliced DOLE® Celery
1/2 cup sliced DOLE® Green
    Onion
1 papaya, peeled, sliced
    (optional)
1 tablespoon cornstarch
1/2 cup water

Drain pineapple, reserve syrup. In
large skillet, brown chicken in
margarine. Drain excess fat.
Combine reserved syrup with
sherry, soy sauce, garlic, ginger
and salt; pour over chicken.
Cover; simmer 30 minutes, turning
chicken once. Remove chicken to
platter.

Add pineapple, bell pepper, celery,
green onion and papaya to skillet.
Dissolve cornstarch in water. Stir
into pan juices. Cook until mixture
boils and thickens. Spoon over
chicken. *Makes 4 servings*

FABULOUS PORK

Sausage Skillet Dinner

12 ounces fully cooked
    smoked pork link
    sausage, cut diagonally
    into 1-inch pieces
2 tablespoons water
1 medium onion
2 small red cooking apples
2 tablespoons butter, divided
12 ounces natural frozen
    potato wedges
1/4 cup cider vinegar
3 tablespoons sugar
1/2 teaspoon caraway seed
2 tablespoons chopped
    parsley

Place sausage and water in large nonstick frying pan; cover tightly and cook over medium heat 8 minutes, stirring occasionally. Meanwhile, cut onion into 12 wedges; core and cut each apple into 8 wedges. Remove sausage to warm platter. Pour off drippings. Cook and stir onion and apples in 1 tablespoon of the butter in same frying pan 4 minutes or until apples are just tender. Remove to sausage platter. Heat remaining 1 tablespoon butter; add potatoes and cook, covered, over medium-high heat 5 minutes or until potatoes are tender and golden brown, stirring occasionally. Combine vinegar, sugar and caraway seed. Reduce heat, return sausage, apple mixture and vinegar mixture to frying pan and cook 1 minute, or until heated through, stirring gently. Sprinkle with parsley. *Makes 4 servings*

Preparation time: 5 minutes
Cooking time: 18 minutes

Favorite recipe from **National Live Stock and Meat Board**

Sausage Skillet Dinner

Saucy Pork and Peppers

Saucy Pork and Peppers

  2 fresh limes
¹/₄ cup 62%-less-sodium soy
     sauce
  1 teaspoon oregano leaves
¹/₂ teaspoon thyme leaves
     Dash cayenne pepper
  4 cloves garlic, crushed
  2 to 3 fresh parsley sprigs
  1 bay leaf
  1 pound pork tenderloin,
     trimmed and cut into
     1-inch cubes
  1 tablespoon olive oil
  1 teaspoon brown sugar
  2 medium onions, each cut
     into 8 pieces
  2 medium tomatoes, each cut
     into 8 pieces and seeded
  1 large red bell pepper, cut
     into 8 pieces
  1 large green bell pepper,
     cut into 8 pieces.

Squeeze juice from limes,
reserving peel. In small bowl,
combine lime juice, lime peel, soy
sauce, oregano, thyme, cayenne
pepper, garlic, parsley and bay
leaf; blend well. Place pork cubes
in plastic bag or non-metal bowl.
Pour lime mixture over pork,
turning to coat. Seal bag or cover
dish; marinate at least 2 hours or
overnight in refrigerator, turning
pork several times.

Remove lime peel, parsley sprigs
and bay leaf from marinade;
discard. Remove pork from
marinade, reserving marinade.
Drain pork well. Heat oil in large
skillet over high heat. Add brown
sugar; stir until sugar is dissolved.
Add pork cubes; cook and stir
about 5 minutes or until pork is
browned. Reduce heat to low. Add
onions, tomatoes, peppers and
reserved marinade; simmer 10 to
15 minutes or until pork is
tender.   *Makes 4 servings*

Favorite recipe from **National Pork
Producers Council**

Pork Sausage and Onion Soup

1 pound fresh pork sausage
2 large yellow onions
2 tablespoons butter or
  margarine
2 cloves garlic, minced
1 teaspoon brown sugar
2 cans (13¾ ounces each)
  single-strength beef
  broth
½ cup dry white wine
½ cup water
1 teaspoon Dijon-style
  mustard
  Freshly ground black
  pepper
1 tablespoon chopped
  parsley

Pinch off 1-inch pieces of sausage
to make approximately 32 free-
form patties; cook sausage patties
(½ at a time) in Dutch oven until
browned on both sides. Remove
patties; keep warm. Pour off
drippings. Cut onions in half
lengthwise; cut into thin slices.
Add butter and onions to same
Dutch oven; cook and stir over
medium-high heat 5 minutes. Add
garlic and sugar; continue to cook
and stir 5 minutes. Add sausage
patties, beef broth, wine, water
and mustard; bring to a boil.
Season with pepper to taste.
Garnish with parsley.

Makes 4 servings

Preparation time: 15 minutes
Cooking time: 30 minutes

Favorite recipe from **National Live
Stock and Meat Board**

Cajun Red Bean and Sausage Casserole

1 pound dried kidney beans
½ pound salt pork or ham,
  diced
3 cups chopped onions
1 cup chopped green onions
1 cup chopped fresh parsley
1 pound smoked sausage, cut
  into ¼-inch slices
1 can (8 ounces) tomato
  sauce
1 tablespoon Worcestershire
  sauce
1 tablespoon LAWRY'S®
  Seasoned Salt
1 teaspoon LAWRY'S®
  Seasoned Pepper
½ teaspoon LAWRY'S® Garlic
  Powder with Parsley
½ teaspoon hot pepper sauce

Rinse beans. Place beans in large,
heavy Dutch oven. Add water to
level 2 inches above beans; let
soak overnight. Add salt pork,
bring to a boil; reduce heat, cover
and simmer 30 minutes. Stir in
remaining ingredients. Cover and
simmer 45 minutes to 1 hour or
until beans are tender.

Makes 8 to 10 servings

Presentation: Serve over hot
cooked rice with a green salad and
crusty bread.

Hint: Heat is more evenly
distributed in a cast iron Dutch
oven.

Classy Cassoulet

6 slices bacon
¼ cup seasoned dry bread
    crumbs
1 pound hot or sweet Italian
    sausage, cut into 1-inch-
    thick slices
1 medium onion, cut into 6
    wedges
3 cloves garlic, finely
    chopped
1 can (16 ounces) sliced
    carrots, drained
1 can (16 ounces) zucchini,
    drained
1 can (8 ounces) stewed
    tomatoes
½ cup chopped celery
1 teaspoon beef-flavored
    instant bouillon granules
1½ teaspoons dried parsley
    flakes
1 bay leaf
2 cans (15 ounces each)
    butter beans, 1 can
    drained, 1 can undrained

Sauté bacon in large skillet, turning until crisp and browned, about 8 minutes. Remove with slotted spoon to paper towels to drain. Set aside skillet with bacon drippings. Combine 2 tablespoons of the bacon drippings with bread crumbs in small bowl. Set aside.

Sauté sausage, onion and garlic in skillet with bacon drippings until sausage is no longer pink, 12 to 15 minutes. Drain off fat, leaving sausage mixture in skillet. Stir carrots, zucchini, tomatoes, celery, bouillon, parsley, bay leaf and 1 can drained butter beans into skillet with sausage. Add can of undrained butter beans. Bring to a boil; lower heat and simmer, uncovered, for 10 minutes or until mixture is heated through and celery is tender. Remove bay leaf.

Place sausage mixture in one 2-quart or 6 individual broiler-proof casseroles. Crumble bacon over top; sprinkle with bread crumb mixture. Broil 5 inches from heat 1 minute or until crumbs are golden; be careful not to burn crumbs. Serve hot with garnish of sliced, canned cranberry sauce.

Makes 6 servings

Favorite recipe from **Canned Food Council**

Classy Cassoulet

Peachy Pork Picante

Peachy Pork Picante

1 pound boneless pork loin,
  cut into 1-inch cubes
1 tablespoon taco
  seasoning mix
2 tablespoons minced
  parsley
2 teaspoons vegetable oil
8 ounces bottled salsa,
  chunky style
1/4 cup peach preserves

Combine taco seasoning and parsley; coat pork cubes with seasoning mixture. Heat oil in heavy skillet over medium-high heat. Add pork, cook and stir to brown, about 3 to 5 minutes. Add salsa and preserves to pan, reduce heat, cook and simmer until tender, about 15 minutes.

Makes 4 servings

Preparation time: 25 minutes

Favorite recipe from **National Pork Producers Council**

Paprika Pork Stew

1 pound boneless pork
  shoulder, cut into 1-inch
  cubes
2 tablespoons all-purpose
  flour
2 tablespoons sweet paprika
1 teaspoon salt
2 tablespoons shortening
1/2 cup water
1 medium onion, cut in half
  lengthwise and sliced
4 small red new potatoes,
  quartered
2 tablespoons water
1/2 cup sour cream

Combine flour, paprika and salt; mix well. Coat pork with flour mixture. Reserve excess flour mixture. Brown pork in shortening in a large skillet or Dutch oven. Pour off drippings. Add 1/2 cup water and onion, cover tightly and cook over low heat for 30 minutes. Add potatoes and continue cooking, covered, 20 to 30 minutes or until pork and potatoes are tender. Combine reserved flour with 2 tablespoons water; stir into pork mixture and cook until thickened, stirring occasionally. Remove from heat and stir in sour cream.

Makes 4 servings

Preparation time: 15 minutes
Cooking time: 60 minutes

Favorite recipe from **National Pork Producers Council**

Family Baked Bean Dinner

1 can (20 oz.) DOLE®
    Pineapple Chunks in
    Juice
½ DOLE® Green Bell Pepper,
    julienne-cut
½ cup chopped onion
1 lb. Polish sausage or
    frankfurters, cut in
    1-inch chunks
⅓ cup brown sugar, packed
1 teaspoon dry mustard
2 cans (16 oz. each) baked
    beans

Drain pineapple, save juice for beverage. Place green pepper and onion in 13×9-inch microwave-safe dish. Cover, microwave on HIGH (100% power) 3 minutes. Add sausage, arranging around edges of dish. Cover; continue microwaving on HIGH 6 minutes. In bowl, combine brown sugar and mustard; stir in beans and pineapple. Add to sausage mixture. Stir to combine. Microwave, uncovered, on HIGH 8 to 10 minutes, stirring after 4 minutes.
Makes 6 servings

Prep time: 15 minutes
Cook time: 20 minutes

Cajun Skillet Hash

1 onion, chopped
2 cloves garlic, crushed
2 tablespoons butter or
    margarine
1 large potato (about
    7 ounces), cooked,
    peeled and chopped
1 can (14½ ounces)
    DEL MONTE® Cajun (or
    Original) Style Stewed
    Tomatoes*
½ teaspoon thyme, crushed
2 cups cooked diced ham
1 green pepper, chopped
    Salt and pepper

In large skillet, cook onion and garlic in butter until tender-crisp. Add potato; cook 2 minutes. Stir in tomatoes and thyme; simmer over medium heat 2 to 3 minutes. Add ham and green pepper. Season with salt and pepper to taste. Simmer, stirring frequently, 3 to 5 minutes. Season with hot pepper sauce. Serve with eggs, if desired.
Makes 6 servings

*If using Original Style Stewed Tomatoes, add a pinch each of cinnamon, ground cloves and cayenne.

Prep time: 8 minutes
Cook time: 14 minutes

Southwestern Stir-Fry

1 pound pork tenderloin, cut
   in quarters lengthwise
   and then sliced ¼ inch
   thick
2 tablespoons dry sherry
2 teaspoons cornstarch
1 teaspoon ground cumin
1 clove garlic, minced
½ teaspoon seasoned salt
1 tablespoon vegetable oil
1 green pepper, seeded and
   cut into strips
1 medium onion, thinly
   sliced
12 cherry tomatoes, halved
   Green chile salsa

Combine sherry, cornstarch,
cumin, garlic and seasoned salt in
medium bowl; add pork slices and
stir to coat. Heat oil over medium-
high heat in heavy skillet. Add pork
mixture and stir-fry about 3 to 4
minutes. Add remaining ingredients
except salsa, cover and simmer 3
to 4 minutes. Serve hot with green
chile salsa.

Makes 4 servings

Favorite recipe from **National Pork
Producers Council**

Swissed Ham and Noodles Casserole

2 tablespoons butter
½ cup chopped onion
½ cup chopped green pepper
1 can (10½ ounces)
   condensed cream of
   mushroom soup
1 cup dairy sour cream
1 package (8 ounces)
   medium noodles, cooked
   and drained
2 cups (8 ounces) shredded
   Wisconsin Swiss cheese
2 cups cubed cooked ham
   (about ¾ pound)

In 1-quart saucepan melt butter;
sauté onion and green pepper.
Remove from heat; stir in soup
and sour cream. In buttered
2-quart casserole layer ⅓ of the
noodles, ⅓ of the Swiss cheese, ⅓
of the ham and ½ soup mixture.
Repeat layers, ending with final ⅓
layer of noodles, cheese and ham.
Bake in preheated 350°F oven 30
to 45 minutes or until heated
through.

Makes 6 to 8 servings

Favorite recipe from **Wisconsin Milk
Marketing Board** © 1992

Southwestern Stir-Fry

Sausage Stuffed Zucchini

Sausage Stuffed Zucchini

    3 medium zucchini (about
        2 pounds)
    12 ounces bulk Italian
        sausage, cooked and
        drained
    1½ cups Wheat CHEX® brand
        cereal, crushed to ½ cup
    ¼ cup water
    1 package (1.5 ounces) dry
        spaghetti sauce mix
    ¼ cup chopped onion
    1 tablespoon olive oil
    1 clove garlic, minced
    ¼ cup chopped green pepper
    2 cups chopped tomatoes
    1 can (8 ounces) tomato
        sauce

Preheat oven to 350°F. Cut zucchini in half lengthwise. Scoop pulp out, leaving ⅛-inch shell; set aside shells. Chop pulp; set aside. In medium bowl combine sausage, cereal, water and 2 tablespoons of the spaghetti sauce mix. Stuff reserved shells with sausage mixture. Place in ungreased 13×9×2-inch baking pan. Bake, covered, 25 to 30 minutes or until hot. In medium saucepan over low heat combine onion, oil and garlic. Cook 2 minutes or until onion is tender. Add green pepper and reserved zucchini pulp. Cook over medium heat 5 minutes or until zucchini is tender, stirring often. Add tomatoes, tomato sauce and remaining spaghetti sauce mix. Cook over low heat 10 minutes or until hot, stirring often. Spoon over stuffed shells. Return to oven 10 minutes or until hot.

Makes 6 servings

Microwave Directions: Prepare zucchini and pulp as above. In medium bowl combine sausage, cereal, water and 2 tablespoons of the spaghetti sauce mix. Stuff reserved shells with sausage mixture. Place in ungreased microwave-safe 13×9×2-inch pan. Microwave on HIGH, covered, 3½ to 4 minutes or until zucchini shells are crisp-tender; set aside. In 3-quart microwave-safe bowl combine onion, oil and garlic. Microwave on HIGH 1 minute or until onion is tender. Add green pepper and reserved zucchini pulp. Microwave on HIGH 2 minutes or until zucchini is tender. Add tomatoes, tomato sauce and remaining spaghetti sauce mix. Microwave on HIGH 3 minutes or until hot, stirring halfway through. Spoon over stuffed shells. Microwave on HIGH 1 minute or until hot.

Chop Suey

      ¼ cup flour
      2 teaspoons salt
      ½ pound cubed veal
      ½ pound cubed pork
      ⅓ cup CRISCO® Shortening
      1 cup chopped onion
      1 cup celery, cut into 1-inch
          pieces
      1 cup beef stock or broth
      ½ cup soy sauce
      2 tablespoons molasses
      1 can (16 ounces) bean
          sprouts, drained
      Hot cooked rice

Combine flour and salt in large plastic food storage bag; add meat cubes and toss lightly to coat. Brown in hot Crisco® in Dutch oven; add onion and continue browning. Stir in celery, beef stock, soy sauce and molasses. Cover and cook over low heat for 25 minutes. Add bean sprouts; cook 15 minutes more. Thicken with additional flour, if necessary. Serve over hot cooked rice.
Makes 4 to 6 servings

Pork Loin Roulade

      4 boneless center pork loin
          slices, about 1 pound
      ½ red bell pepper, cut into
          strips
      ½ green bell pepper, cut into
          strips
      1 teaspoon vegetable oil
      ⅔ cup orange juice
      ⅔ cup bottled barbecue sauce
      1 tablespoon prepared Dijon-
          style mustard

Place pork slices between 2 pieces of plastic wrap. Pound with mallet to about ¼-inch thickness.

Place several red and green pepper strips crosswise on each pork portion; roll up jelly-roll style. Secure rolls with wooden toothpicks.

In nonstick skillet, brown pork rolls in vegetable oil. Drain fat from pan. Combine orange juice, barbecue sauce and mustard; add to skillet. Bring mixture to boiling; reduce heat. Cover and simmer 10 to 12 minutes or until pork is tender. Remove toothpicks to serve.   *Makes 4 servings*

Preparation time: 20 minutes
Cooking time: 12 minutes

Favorite recipe from **National Pork Producers Council**

Pork Loin Roulade

Sesame Pork with Broccoli

1 can (14½ ounces) chicken
    broth
2 tablespoons cornstarch
1 tablespoon soy sauce
4 green onions and tops,
    finely diced
1 pound pork tenderloin,
    trimmed
1 tablespoon vegetable oil
1 clove garlic, minced
1½ pounds fresh broccoli, cut
    into bite-size pieces
    (about 7 cups)
2 tablespoons sliced
    pimiento, drained
2 tablespoons sesame seed,
    lightly toasted

In small bowl, combine chicken broth, cornstarch and soy sauce; blend well. Stir in green onions; set aside. Cut pork tenderloin lengthwise into quarters; cut each quarter into bite-sized pieces. Heat oil in wok or heavy skillet over medium-high heat. Add pork and garlic; stir-fry 3 to 4 minutes or until pork is tender. Remove pork; keep warm. Add broccoli and broth mixture to wok. Cover and simmer over low heat 8 minutes. Add cooked pork and pimiento; cook just until mixture is hot, stirring frequently. Sprinkle with sesame seed. Serve immediately.
Makes 6 servings

Favorite recipe from **National Pork Producers Council**

Pork Cutlets with Garden Vegetables

1½ pounds pork cutlets
2 teaspoons vegetable oil
2½ cups peeled, chopped
    fresh tomatoes
1 can (8 ounces) tomato
    sauce
½ cup chopped onion
¼ cup chopped fresh chiles
    or 4-ounce can diced
    green chiles
1 clove garlic, minced
2 tablespoons fresh lime
    juice
½ teaspoon salt
¼ teaspoon ground cumin
1 cup julienne-cut carrots
1 cup julienne-cut zucchini
¼ cup raisins
¼ cup slivered almonds

Heat oil in nonstick frypan. Brown pork cutlets over medium-high heat. Stir in tomatoes, tomato sauce, onion, chiles, garlic, lime juice, salt and cumin. Cover; simmer 20 minutes. Stir in carrots, zucchini and raisins. Cover; simmer 10 minutes longer or until vegetables are tender. Stir in almonds.   *Makes 6 servings*

Preparation time: 15 minutes
Cooking time: 30 minutes

Favorite recipe from **National Pork Producers Council**

Sesame Pork with Broccoli

Pineapple Ham Stir-Fry

1 can (20 oz.) DOLE®
    Pineapple Chunks in
    Juice
1 clove garlic, pressed
1 tablespoon finely chopped
    ginger
1 tablespoon vegetable oil
½ yellow onion, sliced
½ DOLE® Green or Red Bell
    Pepper, julienne-cut
⅓ cup chicken broth
1 tablespoon cornstarch
1 tablespoon soy sauce
1 tablespoon sherry
½ lb. cooked ham,
    julienne-cut
½ lb. sugar peas
½ lb. bean sprouts
    Hot cooked rice

Drain pineapple; save juice for beverage. In large skillet or wok, sauté garlic and ginger in oil. Add onion and green pepper, sauté 2 minutes. Combine broth, cornstarch, soy sauce and sherry; stir into skillet. Add ham, sugar peas, bean sprouts and pineapple to skillet. Cook and stir until vegetables are tender-crisp, 3 to 4 minutes. Serve with rice.   *Makes 4 servings*

Prep time: 15 minutes
Cook time: 15 minutes

Sage and Rosemary Pork Stew

2 pounds boneless pork
    shoulder roast, cut into
    ¾-inch cubes
1 tablespoon vegetable oil
2 cans (14½ ounces each)
    chicken broth
1 cup water
½ cup sliced green onions
1 tablespoon minced fresh
    rosemary *or* 1 teaspoon
    dried rosemary
1 teaspoon minced fresh
    sage *or* ⅛ teaspoon
    dried sage
¼ teaspoon salt
⅛ teaspoon pepper
2 cups cubed, unpeeled new
    potatoes
½ pound fresh green beans,
    cut up
⅓ cup all-purpose flour
⅔ cup half-and-half

Heat oil in Dutch oven. Brown pork cubes over medium-high heat. Stir in broth, water, onions and seasonings. Bring to a boil; reduce heat. Simmer uncovered for 20 minutes. Stir in potatoes and beans; simmer 15 to 20 minutes or until tender. Combine flour and half-and-half; mix until smooth. Gradually stir into stew. Cook and stir until thickened.
        Makes 6 servings

Preparation time: 15 minutes
Cooking time: 45 minutes

Favorite recipe from **National Pork Producers Council**

Pork Valenciana

Pork Valenciana

1½ pounds boneless pork loin,
    cut into ¾-inch cubes
2 tablespoons olive oil,
    divided
2 yellow onions, peeled and
    chopped
1 green pepper, seeded and
    chopped
2 cloves garlic, minced
1 8-ounce can whole
    tomatoes, undrained
½ teaspoon salt
1 bay leaf
¼ teaspoon pepper
4 cups water
2 cups uncooked rice
2 chicken bouillon cubes
½ cup sherry (optional)
⅛ teaspoon saffron threads
1 cup peas
1 small jar pimientos,
    drained
12 green olives

Brown pork in 1 tablespoon of the oil over medium-high heat in large skillet; remove. Add onions, green pepper, garlic and remaining 1 tablespoon oil. Continue cooking until slightly brown, about 5 minutes. Return pork to pan and stir in tomatoes, salt, bay leaf and pepper. Add water, rice, bouillon and sherry. Dissolve saffron in small amount of water and add to pan. Bring to boil, cover and simmer over low heat 15 minutes. Remove bay leaf. Garnish with peas, pimientos and olives.

Makes 8 servings

Preparation time: 15 minutes
Cooking time: 20 minutes

Favorite recipe from **National Pork Producers Council**

Tuscany Sausage and Rice Skillet

Tuscany Sausage and Rice Skillet

¾ pound Italian sausage, cut
    into 1-inch slices, casings
    removed
1 medium onion, cut into
    thin wedges
1 clove garlic, minced
1½ cups thin red and green
    bell pepper strips
1⅓ cups chicken broth
¼ teaspoon salt
1½ cups UNCLE BEN'S® Rice In
    An Instant
2 tablespoons grated
    Parmesan cheese

Cook sausage with onion and garlic in 10-inch skillet until sausage is cooked through. Pour off all but 1 tablespoon drippings. Add pepper strips, broth and salt. Bring to a boil. Stir in rice; cover and remove from heat. Let stand 5 minutes or until all liquid is absorbed. Sprinkle with cheese.

Makes 4 servings

Pork Ball Stir-Fry

Boiling water
1 package (8 ounces)
    transparent Chinese
    noodles
1 pound ground pork
1 cup cracker crumbs
1 can (8 ounces) water
    chestnuts, drained and
    chopped
6 tablespoons soy sauce,
    divided
1 egg, beaten
1½ tablespoons grated ginger
    root, divided
1 clove garlic, minced
¼ cup almond or vegetable
    oil
1 cup diagonally sliced
    celery
¼ cup cider vinegar
2 tablespoons sugar
1 teaspoon grated orange
    peel
½ teaspoon red pepper flakes
1 cup sliced green onions
1 cup toasted whole almonds
2 tomatoes, cut into wedges
½ cup cilantro leaves

Pour boiling water over noodles;
let stand 2 to 3 minutes; drain and
set aside. Combine pork, cracker
crumbs, water chestnuts, 2
tablespoons of the soy sauce, the
egg, 1 tablespoon of the ginger
root and garlic; mix well. Shape
into 24 meatballs. Brown meatballs
in hot oil, cooking 4 to 5 minutes.
Add celery and sauté. Combine
remaining 4 tablespoons soy sauce,

½ tablespoon ginger, vinegar,
sugar, orange peel and red pepper
flakes. Pour into wok or skillet
and add noodles; heat through.
Toss with green onions, almonds,
tomatoes and cilantro.

Makes 6 servings

Favorite recipe from **Almond Board
of California**

Pork Strips Florentine

1 pound boneless pork strips
1 package (6 ounces)
    seasoned long grain and
    wild rice mix, uncooked
1⅔ cups hot water
1 can (2.8 ounces) DURKEE®
    French Fried Onions
¼ teaspoon DURKEE® Garlic
    Powder
1 package (10 ounces) frozen
    chopped spinach, thawed
    and well drained
2 tablespoons diced
    pimiento (optional)
½ cup (2 ounces) shredded
    Swiss cheese

Preheat oven to 375°F. In 8×12-
inch baking dish, combine pork
strips, rice, contents of rice
seasoning packet, hot water,
½ can Durkee® French Fried
Onions and garlic powder. Bake,
covered, for 30 minutes. Stir
spinach and pimiento into meat
mixture. Bake, covered, 10 minutes
or until pork and rice are done.
Top with cheese and remaining
onions; bake, uncovered, 3
minutes or until onions are golden
brown.

Makes 4 servings

SPLENDID SEAFOOD

Paella

1 tablespoon olive oil
½ pound chicken breast
    cubes
1 cup uncooked rice*
1 medium onion, chopped
1 clove garlic, minced
1½ cups chicken broth
1 can (8 ounces) stewed
    tomatoes, chopped,
    reserving liquid
½ teaspoon paprika
⅛ to ¼ teaspoon ground red
    pepper
⅛ teaspoon ground saffron
½ pound medium shrimp,
    peeled and deveined
1 small red pepper, cut into
    strips
1 small green pepper, cut
    into strips
½ cup frozen green peas

*If using medium grain rice, use
1¼ cups of broth; if using
parboiled rice, use 1¾ cups of
broth.

Heat oil in Dutch oven over medium-high heat until hot. Add chicken and stir until browned. Add rice, onion, and garlic. Cook, stirring, until onion is tender and rice is lightly browned. Add broth, tomatoes, tomato liquid, paprika, ground red pepper, and saffron. Bring to a boil; stir. Reduce heat; cover and simmer 10 minutes. Add shrimp, pepper strips, and peas. Cover and simmer 10 minutes or until rice is tender and liquid is absorbed.   *Makes 6 servings*

Favorite recipe from **USA Rice Council**

Paella

Oriental Seafood Stir-Fry

½ cup water
3 tablespoons REALEMON® Lemon Juice from Concentrate
3 tablespoons soy sauce
1 tablespoon brown sugar
1 tablespoon cornstarch
¾ cup sliced fresh mushrooms
¾ cup diced red bell pepper
1 medium onion, cut into wedges
2 ounces fresh pea pods
1 tablespoon vegetable oil
½ pound imitation crab blend, flaked
  Shredded napa, hot cooked pasta or rice noodles

Combine water, ReaLemon® brand, soy sauce, sugar and cornstarch. In large skillet, cook and stir mushrooms, red pepper, onion and pea pods in oil until tender-crisp; remove. Add soy mixture; cook and stir until slightly thickened. Return vegetables along with crab blend to skillet; heat through. Serve with shredded napa, hot cooked pasta or rice noodles. Refrigerate leftovers.

Makes 4 servings

Oriental Seafood Stir-Fry

Hasty Bouillabaisse

5 green onions, thinly sliced
$^1/_2$ cup chopped green pepper
1 clove garlic, minced
2 tablespoons minced
　　parsley
2 tablespoons olive or
　　vegetable oil
1 can (14$^1/_2$ ounces) stewed
　　or whole tomatoes
1 cup red wine
$^3/_4$ teaspoon dried thyme
　　leaves
$^1/_4$ teaspoon dried rosemary,
　　crushed
$^1/_4$ teaspoon TABASCO® Sauce
1 can (16 ounces) mixed
　　vegetables or peas and
　　carrots *or* 2 cans
　　(8 ounces each) other
　　vegetables (beans, corn,
　　carrots, peas, etc.)
1 can (7 ounces) tuna,
　　drained and flaked
1 can (6 ounces) crabmeat,
　　flaked and cartilage
　　removed
1 can (6 ounces) minced
　　clams, drained
1 can (4$^1/_4$ ounces) shrimp,
　　rinsed and drained

In large saucepan, cook onions, green pepper, garlic and parsley in oil over medium heat until tender. Add tomatoes, wine and seasonings. Simmer 10 minutes. Add vegetables and seafood. Simmer 10 minutes more or until heated through.

Makes 6 to 8 servings

Hasty Bouillabaisse

Tuna Skillet

$^1/_4$ cup CRISCO® Shortening
$^2/_3$ cup chopped onion
1 small green pepper,
　　slivered (about $^1/_2$ cup)
1 can (10$^3/_4$ ounces)
　　condensed tomato soup
2 teaspoons soy sauce
2 to 3 tablespoons brown
　　sugar
1 teaspoon grated lemon
　　peel
3 tablespoons lemon juice
2 cans (6$^1/_2$ or 7 ounces
　　each) tuna, drained
　　Hot cooked rice
　　Red pepper rings
　　(optional)

Melt Crisco® in large heavy skillet over medium heat. Stir in onion and green pepper. Cook until almost tender, stirring occasionally. Mix in tomato soup, soy sauce, brown sugar, lemon peel and lemon juice. Bring to boiling; simmer for 5 minutes. Mix in tuna, separating into small pieces. Heat. Serve with hot cooked rice. Garnish with red pepper rings.

Makes 4 to 6 servings

Dilled Salmon Supper

1 bottle (8 ounces) clam
    juice
½ cup dry vermouth
½ cup UNCLE BEN'S®
    CONVERTED® Brand
    Rice, uncooked
1 tablespoon lime juice
1 clove garlic, crushed
2 teaspoons chopped fresh
    dill or ½ teaspoon dried
    dillweed
⅛ teaspoon freshly ground
    black pepper
2 salmon steaks, ¾-inch
    thick* (about ¾ pound)
½ cup frozen peas, thawed
¼ cup plain low-fat yogurt
    Paprika

Bring clam juice and vermouth to
a boil in 10-inch skillet. Stir in
rice, lime juice, garlic, dill and
pepper. Arrange salmon steaks on
top. Cover and simmer 20
minutes. Remove from heat.
Gently stir peas into rice. Let stand
covered until all liquid is
absorbed, about 5 minutes. Top
salmon with yogurt and sprinkle
with paprika.

Makes 2 servings

*Haddock, halibut or red snapper
fillets, ½- to ¾-inch thick, may be
substituted.

Tuna in Red Pepper Sauce

2 cups chopped red bell
    peppers (about
    2 peppers)
½ cup chopped onion
1 clove garlic, minced
2 tablespoons vegetable oil
¼ cup dry red or white wine
¼ cup chicken broth
2 teaspoons sugar
¼ teaspoon pepper
1 red bell pepper, slivered
    and cut into ½-inch
    pieces
1 yellow or green bell
    pepper, slivered and cut
    into ½-inch pieces
½ cup julienne-strip carrots
1 can (9¼ ounces)
    STARKIST® Tuna, drained
    and broken into chunks
    Hot cooked pasta or rice

In skillet sauté chopped bell
peppers, onion and garlic in oil
for 5 minutes, or until vegetables
are very tender. In blender or food
processor container place vegetable
mixture; cover and process until
puréed. Return to pan; stir in
wine, chicken broth, sugar and
pepper. Keep warm. In 2-quart
saucepan steam bell pepper pieces
and carrots over simmering water
for 5 minutes. Stir steamed
vegetables into sauce with tuna;
cook for 2 minutes, or until
heated through. Serve tuna
mixture over pasta or rice.

Makes 4 to 5 servings

Preparation time: 20 minutes

Tuna in Red Pepper Sauce

Autumn Seafood Bake

Preheat oven to 350°F. Cut squash in half lengthwise; remove seeds. Place cut-side down in 3-quart baking dish. Add ½ inch water to dish. Bake 30 to 35 minutes or until squash is tender when pierced with a fork. Remove squash; pour water from dish. In large bowl combine Worcestershire, onion, celery, olives, shrimp and crabmeat; mix well. Add cheese and cereals, stirring until well combined. Fill each squash half with 1 cup mixture. Place in baking dish. Bake 15 to 20 minutes or until heated through.

Makes 6 servings

Autumn Seafood Bake

 3 acorn squash (about
  4 pounds)
¼ cup white wine
  Worcestershire sauce
¼ cup chopped onion
¼ cup sliced celery
¼ cup sliced ripe olives
 1 can (4¼ ounces) medium
  shrimp, rinsed and
  drained
 1 can (6½ ounces)
  crabmeat, drained
 1 cup (4 ounces) shredded
  Cheddar cheese
1½ cups Corn CHEX® brand
  cereal
1½ cups Wheat CHEX® brand
  cereal

Shrimp and Vegetable Stir-Fry

¾ pound raw medium
  shrimp, peeled and
  deveined
 3 teaspoons cornstarch,
  divided
⅛ teaspoon ground ginger
  Dash garlic powder
½ pound fresh broccoli
 5 cups water, divided
 1 tablespoon sesame seed
  (optional)
 4 tablespoons BUTTER
  FLAVOR CRISCO®,
  divided
½ teaspoon instant chicken
  bouillon granules
 1 package (6 ounces) frozen
  pea pods, thawed
  Hot cooked rice

Mix shrimp, 1 teaspoon of the cornstarch, ginger and garlic powder in medium bowl. Cover and refrigerate until ready to use. Cut thin slices (¼ to ½ inch) off stalk ends of broccoli to remove tough part; discard thin slices. Cut large stalks in half or quarters and then into ¾-inch pieces; cut heads into flowerets. Heat 4 cups of the water to boiling in 2-quart saucepan. Add broccoli. Cover and cook 1 minute; remove from heat. Drain; rinse under cold water, drain again and set aside.

Cook sesame seed in small skillet over moderate heat until golden brown, stirring frequently. Remove from heat; set aside.

Melt 2 tablespoons Butter Flavor Crisco® in large skillet over moderate heat. Add shrimp mixture. Cook and stir until shrimp are opaque and white. Remove; set aside.

Blend remaining 1 cup cold water, 2 teaspoons cornstarch and bouillon granules in small bowl. Set aside.

In same large skillet melt remaining 2 tablespoons Butter Flavor Crisco®. Add broccoli. Cook and stir over moderate heat until tender. Add pea pods. Cook and stir 1 minute longer. Add cornstarch mixture. Cook and stir until mixture begins to bubble. Add shrimp. Cook and stir until mixture thickens and bubbles. Sprinkle with sesame seed before serving. Serve over rice, if desired.

Makes 4 to 6 servings

Lemon Fish Roll-Ups

1 cup cooked rice
1 (10-ounce) package frozen chopped broccoli, thawed and well drained
1 cup (4 ounces) shredded Cheddar cheese
⅓ cup margarine or butter, melted
⅓ cup REALEMON® Lemon Juice from Concentrate
½ teaspoon salt
¼ teaspoon pepper
8 fish fillets, fresh or frozen, thawed (about 2 pounds)
Paprika

Preheat oven to 375°F. In medium bowl, combine rice, broccoli and cheese. Combine margarine, ReaLemon® brand, salt and pepper; add ¼ cup margarine mixture to broccoli mixture. Place equal amounts of mixture on fillets; roll up. Place seam-side down in shallow baking dish; pour remaining margarine mixture over roll-ups. Bake 20 minutes or until fish flakes with fork. Garnish with paprika. Refrigerate leftovers.

Makes 8 servings

Lemon Fish Roll-Ups

Crab and Rice Primavera

1½ cups BIRDS EYE® Farm Fresh Broccoli, Green Beans, Pearl Onions and Red Peppers
¼ cup water
1⅓ cups milk
1 pound imitation crabmeat or fresh or frozen crabmeat
2 tablespoons butter or margarine
1 teaspoon garlic salt
¾ teaspoon dried basil leaves
1½ cups MINUTE® Rice, uncooked
½ cup grated Parmesan cheese

Bring vegetables and water to a boil in medium saucepan, stirring occasionally. Reduce heat; cover and simmer 3 minutes.

Add milk, imitation crabmeat, butter, garlic salt and basil. Bring to a full boil. Stir in rice and cheese. Cover, remove from heat. Let stand 5 minutes. Fluff with fork.   *Makes 4 servings*

Savory Salmon Chowder

1 can (15½ ounces) salmon
5 slices bacon, diced
½ cup chopped onion
½ cup chopped green pepper
2 cups diced potatoes
1 package (10 ounces) frozen mixed vegetables
2½ cups water
2 chicken bouillon cubes
1 can (13 ounces) evaporated milk
1 can (8½ ounces) cream-style corn
½ teaspoon salt
½ teaspoon celery salt
½ teaspoon dill weed
⅛ teaspoon pepper
1 tablespoon minced parsley

Drain salmon, reserving liquid; flake and debone. Sauté bacon, onion and green pepper in large skillet. Add potatoes, mixed vegetables, water and bouillon cubes. Cover and simmer 10 to 12 minutes or until vegetables are tender. Add salmon with liquid, evaporated milk, corn and seasonings except parsley; heat through. Sprinkle with parsley before serving.

Makes 6 servings

Favorite recipe from **Alaska Seafood Marketing Institute**

Crab and Rice Primavera

Louisiana Tomato-Rice Gumbo

    1 whole boned chicken
        breast, cut into pieces
    2 tablespoons margarine
    ½ cup chopped onion
    ½ cup chopped green pepper
    ½ cup chopped celery
    1 garlic clove, minced
    1 package (10 ounces) frozen
        okra, thawed and sliced
    1 can (16 ounces) crushed
        tomatoes
    1 can (13¾ ounces) chicken
        broth
    1 small bay leaf
    ½ teaspoon sugar
    ¼ teaspoon salt
    ⅛ teaspoon thyme leaves
        Dash of pepper
    ½ pound raw shrimp, cleaned
    1⅓ cups MINUTE® Rice,
        uncooked

Cook and stir chicken in hot margarine in large skillet until lightly browned. Stir in onion, green pepper, celery and garlic; cook until tender.

Add okra, tomatoes, broth and seasonings. Bring to a boil. Reduce heat; cover and simmer 5 minutes, stirring occasionally. Add shrimp and cook 5 minutes. Remove bay leaf. Stir in rice. Cover; remove from heat. Let stand 5 minutes.

Makes 8 servings

New Potato Stuffed Trout

    1½ pounds red new potatoes,
        cooked
    ½ cup chopped fresh parsley
    ¼ cup capers
    ¼ cup black or Greek olives,
        sliced
    3 tablespoons olive oil,
        divided
    ¾ teaspoon salt
    ½ teaspoon freshly ground
        black pepper
    4 CLEAR SPRINGS® Brand
        Idaho Rainbow Trout,
        whole, boned (8 ounces
        each)
    4 teaspoons fresh lemon
        juice
        Salt and freshly ground
        pepper
    ½ cup white wine or
        vermouth
    2 lemons, thinly sliced

Cut potatoes into large cubes. Combine with parsley, capers, olives, 2 tablespoons of the oil, ¾ teaspoon salt and ½ teaspoon pepper in large bowl. Mix well; set aside. Sprinkle inside of each trout with lemon juice, salt and pepper. Stuff each trout with ¼ of potato mixture. Pour wine into baking pan. Place stuffed trout in pan. Brush trout with remaining 1 tablespoon oil. Top with lemon slices. Cover pan with foil and bake at 400°F for about 15 minutes until trout flakes easily with a fork. *Makes 4 servings*

Louisiana Tomato-Rice Gumbo

Rainbow Trout Santa Fe

2 tablespoons olive oil
4 CLEAR SPRINGS® Brand
    Idaho Rainbow Trout
    fillets (4 ounces each)
2 teaspoons butter
2 cloves garlic, minced
¼ cup chopped green onion
1 small tomato, peeled,
    seeded and diced
½ cup fresh or frozen whole
    corn kernels
½ cup snow peas, cut in half
    diagonally
2 tablespoons chopped
    cilantro or parsley
1 to 1½ teaspoons finely
    chopped jalapeño
    pepper*
1 teaspoon fresh lemon juice
¼ teaspoon salt
    Dash white pepper
¼ cup heavy cream
    Tortilla chips

Heat oil over medium-high heat in large skillet. Sauté trout 1 to 2 minutes on each side or until fish flakes easily; remove. Melt butter over medium heat. Sauté garlic and green onion, about 1 minute. Add tomato, corn, snow peas, cilantro, jalapeño, lemon juice, salt and pepper. Simmer about 2 to 3 minutes. Stir in cream; gently simmer about 1 minute more. Top trout with sauce. Serve immediately with tortilla chips.

Makes 4 servings

* Wear rubber gloves when working with jalapeño peppers and wash hands with warm soapy water. Avoid touching face or eyes.

Old-Fashioned Tuna Noodle Casserole

¼ cup plain dry bread
    crumbs
3 tablespoons butter or
    margarine, melted and
    divided
1 tablespoon finely chopped
    parsley
½ cup chopped onion
½ cup chopped celery
1 cup water
1 cup milk
1 package LIPTON® Noodles
    & Sauce—Butter
2 cans (6½ ounces each)
    tuna, drained and flaked

In small bowl, thoroughly combine bread crumbs, 1 tablespoon of the butter and the parsley; set aside.

In medium saucepan, cook onion and celery in remaining 2 tablespoons butter over medium heat, stirring occasionally, 2 minutes or until onion is tender. Add water and milk; bring to a boil. Stir in noodles & butter sauce. Continue boiling over medium heat, stirring occasionally, 8 minutes or until noodles are tender. Stir in tuna. Turn into greased 1-quart casserole, then top with bread crumb mixture. Broil until bread crumbs are golden.

Makes about 4 servings

Baja Fish and Rice Bake

Baja Fish and Rice Bake

3 tablespoons vegetable oil
¾ cup chopped onion
½ cup chopped celery
1 clove garlic, minced
½ cup rice, uncooked
3½ cups (two 14½-ounce cans)
   CONTADINA® Stewed
   Tomatoes, cut up
1 teaspoon lemon pepper
½ teaspoon salt
⅛ teaspoon cayenne pepper
1 pound fish fillets (any firm
   white fish)
¼ cup finely chopped fresh
   parsley
Lemon slices (optional)

Preheat oven to 400°F. In large skillet, heat oil; sauté onion, celery and garlic. Stir in rice; sauté about 5 minutes, or until rice browns slightly. Add tomatoes with juice, lemon pepper, salt and cayenne pepper. Place fish in 12×7½×2-inch baking dish. Spoon rice mixture over fish. Cover with foil; bake 45 to 50 minutes or until rice is tender. Allow to stand 5 minutes before serving. Sprinkle with parsley. Garnish with lemon slices, if desired.   *Makes 6 servings*

"Dearhearts" Seafood Bisque

2 tablespoons olive oil
1 onion, finely chopped
3 pounds fresh baby artichokes, outer leaves removed, leaf tips trimmed and cut into quarters
2 cups chicken broth
½ cup white wine
1 pound mixed shellfish (shrimp, crab, scallops), cleaned and shells removed
1 cup heavy cream
2 tablespoons chopped parsley
1 teaspoon salt
½ teaspoon ground nutmeg
¼ teaspoon white pepper

Heat oil in large saucepan; add onion and cook gently for 5 minutes or until softened. Add artichokes, broth and wine. Cover and simmer 20 to 30 minutes or until artichokes are tender and a leaf pulls away easily. Process mixture in food processor or blender until smooth. Return soup to saucepan. Stir in shellfish, cream, parsley, salt, nutmeg and pepper. Simmer very gently, uncovered, over low heat 5 to 10 minutes. *Do not boil* or shellfish will become tough.

Makes 6 servings

Favorite recipe from **Castroville Artichoke Festival**

Shrimp Pilaf

6 slices bacon, diced
1 cup chopped onion
¾ cup regular long-grain rice, uncooked
1 (13¾-ounce) can COLLEGE INN® Chicken Broth
2 medium tomatoes, chopped
2 teaspoons lemon juice
¼ teaspoon ground black pepper
⅛ teaspoon ground red pepper
1 pound medium shrimp, peeled and deveined*
Parsley (optional)

In large skillet, over medium heat, cook bacon until crisp; remove from pan and set aside, reserving 1 tablespoon drippings. In same skillet sauté onion in reserved drippings until tender; stir in rice, broth, tomatoes, lemon juice and peppers; bring to a boil. Cover; reduce heat and simmer 25 minutes or until rice is tender. Stir in shrimp and bacon; cook and stir until shrimp is cooked and pink, about 5 minutes. Garnish with parsley if desired.

Makes 4 servings

*2 (6½-ounce) cans shrimp can be substituted.

"Dearhearts" Seafood Bisque

Garlic Shrimp with Noodles

Garlic Shrimp with Noodles

4 tablespoons butter, divided
¼ cup finely chopped onion
2 cups water
1 package LIPTON® Noodles
    & Sauce—Butter & Herb
2 tablespoons olive oil
1 tablespoon finely chopped
    garlic
1 pound raw medium
    shrimp, cleaned
1 can (14 ounces) artichoke
    hearts, drained and
    halved
¼ cup finely chopped parsley
    Pepper to taste

In medium saucepan, melt 2 tablespoons of the butter; add onion and cook until tender. Add water and bring to a boil. Stir in noodles & butter & herb sauce; continue boiling over medium heat, stirring occasionally, 8 minutes or until noodles are tender.

Meanwhile, in large skillet, heat remaining 2 tablespoons butter with olive oil; cook garlic over medium-high heat 30 seconds. Add shrimp and artichokes; cook, stirring occasionally, 3 minutes or until shrimp turn pink. Stir in parsley and pepper. To serve, combine shrimp mixture with hot noodles. Garnish, if desired, with watercress.

Makes about 4 servings

Microwave Directions: In 2-quart microwave-safe casserole, microwave 2 tablespoons of the butter with onion, uncovered, at HIGH (Full Power) 2 minutes or until tender. Stir in water and noodles & butter & herb sauce and microwave 11 minutes or until noodles are tender. Stir, then cover and set aside.

In 1-quart microwave-safe casserole or 9-inch glass pie plate, microwave remaining 2 tablespoons butter, olive oil and garlic at HIGH (Full Power) 2 minutes. Stir in shrimp and artichokes and microwave 3 minutes or until shrimp are almost pink, stirring once; stir in parsley and pepper. Combine shrimp mixture with noodles and microwave, covered, 1 minute or until heated through. Let stand, covered, 2 minutes.

Herb-Baked Fish & Rice

1½ cups hot chicken broth
 ½ cup uncooked regular rice
 ¼ teaspoon DURKEE® Italian
    Seasoning
 ¼ teaspoon DURKEE® Garlic
    Powder
 1 package (10 ounces) frozen
    chopped broccoli,
    thawed and drained
 1 can (2.8 ounces) DURKEE®
    French Fried Onions
 1 tablespoon grated
    Parmesan cheese
 1 pound unbreaded fish
    fillets, thawed if frozen
    DURKEE® Paprika
    (optional)
 ½ cup (2 ounces) shredded
    Cheddar cheese

Preheat oven to 375°F. In 12×8-inch baking dish, combine hot broth, uncooked rice and seasonings. Bake, covered, for 10 minutes. Top with broccoli, ½ can Durkee® French Fried Onions and the Parmesan cheese. Place fish fillets diagonally down center of dish; sprinkle fish lightly with paprika. Bake, covered, for 20 to 25 minutes or until fish flakes easily with fork. Top fish with Cheddar cheese and remaining onions; bake, uncovered, 3 minutes or until onions are golden brown.   *Makes 3 to 4 servings*

Microwave Directions: In 12×8-inch microwave-safe dish, prepare rice mixture as above, except reduce broth to 1¼ cups. Cook, covered, on HIGH 5 minutes, stirring halfway through cooking time. Stir in broccoli, ½ *can* Durkee® French Fried Onions and Parmesan cheese. Arrange fish fillets in single layer on top of rice mixture; sprinkle fish lightly with paprika. Cook, covered, on MEDIUM (50%) 18 to 20 minutes or until fish flakes easily with fork and rice is done. Rotate dish halfway through cooking time. Top fish with Cheddar cheese and remaining onions; cook, uncovered, on HIGH 1 minute or until cheese melts. Let stand 5 minutes.

Herb-Baked Fish & Rice

PASTA PLUS

Italian Baked Frittata

1 cup broccoli flowerets
½ cup sliced mushrooms
½ red pepper, cut into rings
2 green onions, sliced into
    1-inch pieces
1 tablespoon BLUE BONNET®
    Margarine
8 eggs
¼ cup GREY POUPON® Dijon
    Mustard or GREY POUPON®
    Country Dijon Mustard
¼ cup water
½ teaspoon Italian seasoning
1 cup shredded Swiss cheese
    (4 ounces)

In 10-inch ovenproof skillet, over medium-high heat, cook broccoli, mushrooms, red pepper and onions in margarine until tender-crisp, about 5 minutes. Remove from heat.

In small bowl, with electric mixer at medium speed, beat eggs, mustard, water and Italian seasoning until foamy; stir in cheese. Pour mixture into skillet over vegetables. Bake at 375°F for 20 to 25 minutes or until set. Serve immediately.

Makes 4 servings

Chicken and Pasta Soup

1 (2½-pound) chicken,
    cut up
1 (46-fluid ounce) can
    COLLEGE INN® Chicken
    Broth
1 (16-ounce) can cut green
    beans, drained
1 (6-ounce) can tomato paste
1 cup uncooked small shell
    macaroni
1 teaspoon dried basil leaves

In large saucepan, over medium-high heat, bring chicken and chicken broth to a boil; reduce heat. Cover; simmer 25 minutes or until chicken is tender. Remove chicken; cool slightly. Add remaining ingredients to broth. Heat to a boil; reduce heat. Cover; simmer 20 minutes or until macaroni is cooked. Meanwhile, remove chicken from bones and cut into bite-size pieces. Add to soup; cook 5 minutes more.

Makes 6 servings

Italian Baked Frittata

*Scandinavian
Salmon-Cheddar Pie*

Heat oven to 425°F. Beat eggs in large bowl; add milk, 2 tablespoons of the parsley, the butter, green onion, 1 tablespoon lemon juice, Worcestershire sauce and mustard; mix well. Fold in cheese and salmon; pour into cooled pie shell. Bake 20 to 25 minutes or until just set and crust is golden brown. Let stand 10 minutes before serving. Combine sour cream, cucumber, remaining 1 tablespoon parsley, dill, remaining 1 teaspoon lemon juice and pepper; mix well. Dollop each serving with sour cream mixture.

Makes 6 servings

Favorite recipe from **Wisconsin Milk Marketing Board** ©1992

Scandinavian Salmon-Cheddar Pie

3 large eggs
¼ cup milk
3 tablespoons chopped parsley, divided
2 tablespoons butter, melted
2 tablespoons minced green onion
1 tablespoon plus 1 teaspoon lemon juice
1 teaspoon Worcestershire sauce
½ teaspoon dry mustard
2 cups (8 ounces) shredded Wisconsin Cheddar cheese
½ pound fresh cooked, flaked salmon *or* 1 can (6½ ounce) salmon, drained, deboned and flaked
1 (9-inch) pie shell, baked and cooled
¾ cup dairy sour cream
¼ cup finely chopped cucumber
1 teaspoon dill weed
⅛ teaspoon ground white pepper

South-of-the-Border Lasagna

1 pound ground beef
½ pound Italian Sausage
1 large onion, chopped
3 tablespoons olive oil, divided
4 (10-ounce) cans spicy tomatoes with chili peppers, drained
3 teaspoons Italian seasoning
2 teaspoons cumin
2 teaspoons seasoned salt
12 corn tortillas, cut into strips
2 eggs
1 pound Wisconsin Ricotta cheese
4 cups (16 ounces) shredded Wisconsin Mozzarella cheese, divided

Preheat oven to 350°F. In skillet brown beef and sausage with onion in 1 tablespoon of the olive oil; drain. Mash tomatoes with fork and add Italian seasoning, cumin and seasoned salt; mix well. Add tomato mixture to beef mixture. Simmer 30 minutes. Meanwhile, grease 12×8×2-inch pan with 1 tablespoon of the olive oil, then line pan with a single layer of tortilla strips. Beat eggs and mix with ricotta cheese and 3 cups of the mozzarella cheese. Spoon ½ of beef mixture over tortilla strips. Add ½ of cheese mixture. Repeat layers of tortilla strips, meat mixture and cheese mixture. Top with final layer of tortilla strips brushed with remaining 1 tablespoon olive oil and sprinkle with remaining mozzarella cheese. Bake 30 minutes or until heated through. Let stand 20 minutes before serving.   *Makes 10 to 12 servings*

Favorite recipe from **Wisconsin Milk Marketing Board** © 1992

Pizza Casserole

- 1 (1-pound) loaf Italian bread, cut into 1-inch slices
- 4 eggs
- 1 (15-ounce) can tomato sauce
- 1¼ cups water
- 1½ teaspoons Italian seasoning
- 1 (3-ounce) package sliced pepperoni
- 1 (8-ounce) package FISHER® Pizza-Mate® Shredded Imitation Mozzarella Cheese

In greased 13×9-inch baking dish, arrange bread slices. In large bowl, beat eggs; mix in tomato sauce, water and Italian seasoning. Pour evenly over bread, moistening completely. Top with pepperoni and Pizza Mate® shreds. Cover; refrigerate 4 hours or overnight. Bake in preheated 350°F oven for 30 minutes or until hot. Refrigerate leftovers.
Makes 8 to 10 servings

Pizza Casserole

Tortellini Primavera

1 cup sliced mushrooms
1/2 cup chopped onion
1 garlic clove, minced
2 tablespoons PARKAY®
    Margarine
1 package (10 ounces)
    BIRDS EYE® Chopped
    Spinach, thawed, well
    drained
1 container (8 ounces)
    PHILADELPHIA BRAND®
    Soft Cream Cheese
1 medium tomato, chopped
1/4 cup milk
1/4 cup (1 ounce) KRAFT®
    100% Grated Parmesan
    Cheese
1 teaspoon Italian seasoning
1/4 teaspoon salt
1/4 teaspoon pepper
8 to 9 ounces fresh or frozen
    cheese-filled tortellini,
    cooked, drained

Cook and stir mushrooms, onion
and garlic in margarine in large
skillet. Add all remaining
ingredients except tortellini; mix
well. Cook until mixture just
begins to boil, stirring
occasionally. Stir in tortellini;
cook until thoroughly heated.
Makes 4 servings

Prep time: 10 minutes
Cooking time: 10 minutes

Cheese Stuffed Green Peppers

6 medium green peppers
1/3 cup chopped onion
2 tablespoons butter
3 cups cooked regular rice
3 cups (12 ounces) shredded
    Wisconsin Cheddar
    cheese
2 tablespoons chopped
    pimiento
1/2 teaspoon salt
    Bacon curls for garnish
    (optional) or imitation
    bacon bits

Cut off tops of green peppers;
remove seeds and membranes.
Precook 5 minutes in boiling
salted water; drain. Sauté onion in
butter until golden. In medium
bowl combine onion, rice,
Cheddar cheese, pimiento and salt;
toss to blend. Spoon into green
peppers, packing down lightly.
Place peppers upright in 10×6-
inch baking dish. Bake in 350°F
oven 25 to 30 minutes or until
heated through. Garnish each with
bacon curl, if desired.
Makes 6 servings

Favorite recipe from **Wisconsin Milk
Marketing Board** ©1992

Tortellini Primavera

Microwave Macaroni and Cheese

Microwave Macaroni and Cheese

2 cups lowfat milk, divided
2 tablespoons MAZOLA®
    Margarine
1 small red pepper, chopped
3 green onions, sliced
1 teaspoon Dijon-style
    mustard
1/2 teaspoon salt
1/4 teaspoon hot pepper sauce
3 tablespoons ARGO® or
    KINGSFORD'S®
    Corn Starch
7 ounces MUELLER'S® Pasta
    Curls, cooked and
    drained
1 package (10 ounces) frozen
    chopped broccoli,
    thawed and drained
2 cups (8 ounces) shredded
    Cheddar cheese
1 cup diced cooked ham

In 2-quart microwavable bowl or casserole combine 1 1/2 cups of the milk, the margarine, red pepper, onions, mustard, salt and hot pepper sauce. Microwave on High (100%), 4 minutes. In small bowl stir remaining 1/2 cup milk and corn starch until smooth. Add to mixture in bowl. Microwave 4 minutes, stirring twice. Stir in pasta, broccoli, cheese and ham. Microwave 4 minutes or until hot. Stir before serving.

Makes 4 servings

Hearty Meatless Chili

1 envelope LIPTON® Onion,
    Onion-Mushroom or
    Beefy Mushroom Recipe
    Soup Mix
4 cups water
1 can (16 ounces) chick peas
    or garbanzo beans,
    rinsed and drained
1 can (16 ounces) red kidney
    beans, rinsed and drained
1 can (14½ ounces) whole
    peeled tomatoes, drained
    and chopped (reserve
    liquid)
1 cup uncooked lentils,
    rinsed
1 large stalk celery, coarsely
    chopped
1 tablespoon chili powder
2 teaspoons ground cumin
1 medium clove garlic,
    finely chopped
¼ teaspoon crushed red
    pepper
    Hot cooked brown or
    regular rice
    Shredded Cheddar cheese

In large saucepan or stockpot, combine all ingredients except rice and cheese. Bring to a boil, then simmer covered 20 minutes or until lentils are almost tender. Remove cover and simmer, stirring occasionally, an additional 30 minutes or until liquid is almost absorbed and lentils are tender. Serve, if desired, over rice and top with shredded cheese.

Makes 6 to 8 servings

Swiss-Bacon Onion Pie

1 cup fine cracker crumbs
    (about 26 crackers)
¼ cup (½ stick) butter,
    melted
6 slices bacon
1 cup chopped onions
2 eggs, slightly beaten
¾ cup dairy sour cream
½ teaspoon salt
    Dash pepper
2 cups (8 ounces) shredded
    Wisconsin Swiss cheese
½ cup (2 ounces) shredded
    Wisconsin Sharp
    Cheddar cheese

Combine cracker crumbs and butter; press onto bottom and side of 8-inch pie plate. Set aside. Cook bacon until crisp. Remove bacon and drain on paper towels; crumble. Pour off all but 2 tablespoons bacon fat; add onion and cook until tender but not brown. Drain.

In large bowl, mix onion with crumbled bacon, eggs, sour cream, salt, pepper and Swiss cheese. Pour mixture into crust. Sprinkle top with Cheddar cheese.

Bake in preheated 375°F oven for 25 to 30 minutes, or until knife inserted half-way between the center and edge of filling comes out clean. Let stand 5 to 10 minutes before serving.

Makes 4 to 6 servings

Favorite recipe from **Wisconsin Milk Marketing Board** ©1992

Vegetable & Cheese Pot Pie

2 tablespoons butter or
  margarine
½ cup sliced green onions
1¾ cups water
1 package LIPTON® Noodles
  & Sauce—Chicken Flavor
1 package (16 ounces) frozen
  mixed vegetables,
  partially thawed
1 cup shredded mozzarella
  cheese (4 ounces)
1 teaspoon prepared mustard
½ cup milk
1 tablespoon all-purpose
  flour
  Salt and pepper to taste
  Pastry for 9-inch single-
  crust pie
1 egg yolk
1 tablespoon water

Preheat oven to 425°F. In large saucepan, melt butter and cook green onions over medium heat 3 minutes or until tender. Add water and bring to a boil. Stir in noodles & chicken flavor sauce and vegetables, then continue boiling over medium heat, stirring occasionally, 7 minutes or until noodles are almost tender. Stir in cheese, mustard and milk blended with flour. Cook over medium heat, stirring frequently, 2 minutes or until thickened. Add salt and pepper.

Turn into greased 1-quart round casserole or soufflé dish, then top with pastry. Press pastry around edge of casserole to seal; trim excess pastry, then flute edges. (Use extra pastry to make decorative shapes.) Brush pastry with egg yolk beaten with water. With tip of knife, make small slits in pastry. Bake 12 minutes or until crust is golden brown.

Makes 4 servings

Turkey Orzo Italiano

¼ pound sliced mushrooms
½ cup sliced green onions
2 tablespoons margarine
2 cups turkey broth or
  reduced-sodium chicken
  broth
1 cup orzo pasta, uncooked
½ teaspoon Italian seasoning
½ teaspoon salt
⅛ teaspoon white pepper
2 cups cubed cooked turkey

In large skillet, over medium-high heat, sauté mushrooms and onions in margarine for 1 minute. Add turkey broth and bring to a boil.

Stir in orzo, Italian seasoning, salt and pepper; bring to a boil. Reduce heat and simmer, covered, 15 minutes or until orzo is tender and liquid has been absorbed. Stir in turkey and heat through.

Makes 4 servings

Favorite recipe from **National Turkey Federation**

Vegetable & Cheese Pot Pie

Mostaccioli and Sausage

Mostaccioli and Sausage

1½ pounds link Italian
    sausage, sliced
1 cup chopped onion
¾ cup chopped green bell
    pepper
2 (26-ounce) jars CLASSICO®
    Pasta Sauce, any flavor
½ cup grated Parmesan
    cheese
1 (1-pound) package
    CREAMETTE®
    Mostaccioli, cooked as
    package directs and
    drained
2 tablespoons olive oil

In large saucepan, brown sausage;
pour off fat. Add onion and green
pepper; cook and stir until tender.
Add pasta sauce and Parmesan
cheese. Bring to a boil; reduce
heat. Cover and simmer 15
minutes, stirring occasionally. Toss
hot cooked mostaccioli with oil.
Serve with sauce. Garnish as
desired. Refrigerate leftovers.
Makes 6 to 8 servings

Classic Stuffed Shells

18 CREAMETTE® Jumbo
    Macaroni Shells, cooked
    as package directs and
    drained
½ pound lean ground beef
⅔ cup chopped onion
1 clove garlic, chopped
1 (26-ounce) jar CLASSICO®
    Di Sicilia (Ripe Olives &
    Mushrooms) Pasta Sauce
1½ teaspoons oregano leaves
1 (15- or 16-ounce) container
    ricotta cheese
2 cups (8 ounces) shredded
    mozzarella cheese
½ cup grated Parmesan
    cheese
1 egg

In skillet, brown meat, onion and
garlic; pour off fat. Stir in pasta
sauce and oregano. In large bowl,
mix ricotta cheese, *1 cup*
mozzarella, Parmesan cheese and
egg. Stuff shells with cheese
mixture. In 13×9-inch baking dish
or 6 individual ramekins, pour
about half the sauce mixture;
arrange stuffed shells in sauce. Top
with remaining sauce; cover. Bake
in preheated 350°F oven 30
minutes. Uncover; sprinkle with
remaining *1 cup* mozzarella. Bake
3 minutes longer. Refrigerate
leftovers.

Makes 6 to 8 servings

Viking Vegetable Cassoulet

4 cups thickly sliced
    mushrooms
2 tablespoons olive oil
2 large onions, thickly sliced
1 large clove garlic, minced
2 medium zucchini, cut into
    1-inch pieces
1½ cups sliced yellow squash
2 cans (16 ounces each)
    white beans, drained
1 can (14½ ounces) plum
    tomatoes, undrained and
    cut up
⅓ cup chopped parsley
1 teaspoon dried basil,
    crushed
½ teaspoon dried oregano,
    crushed
½ cup bread crumbs
2 tablespoons melted butter
2 cups shredded Jarlsberg
    cheese

In large, deep skillet, brown
mushrooms in oil. Add onions and
garlic; sauté 5 minutes. Add
zucchini and yellow squash; sauté
until vegetables are crisp-tender.
Blend in beans, tomatoes with
juice, parsley, basil and oregano.
Spoon into 2-quart baking dish.
Sprinkle bread crumbs combined
with butter around edge. Bake at
350°F for 20 minutes. Top with
cheese; bake 20 minutes longer.
Makes 6 to 8 servings

Favorite recipe from **Norseland
Foods, Inc.**

Vegetable-Ricotta Pie

2 tablespoons vegetable oil
1 cup shredded carrots
1 cup sliced fresh
  mushrooms
1/2 cup finely chopped onion
2 garlic cloves, minced
  (optional)
3/4 cup fresh or thawed and
  drained frozen chopped
  spinach
3 eggs
1 container (15 ounces)
  POLLY-O® Ricotta Cheese
3/4 teaspoon salt
1/4 teaspoon ground nutmeg
1 unbaked 9-inch quiche or
  pie shell

Preheat oven to 425°F. In medium skillet, heat oil over medium heat. In hot oil, sauté carrots, mushrooms, onion and garlic 3 to 5 minutes until tender-crisp. Stir in spinach and cook 1 minute longer; remove from heat.

In medium bowl, beat eggs. Stir in ricotta, salt and nutmeg until well blended. Stir in vegetable mixture; mix well.

Pour mixture into pie shell. Bake 10 minutes. *Reduce oven temperature to 375°F.* Bake 35 minutes longer or until filling is set and crust is golden brown. Serve hot or refrigerate to serve cold or at room temperature.
Makes 6 servings

Preparation time: 20 minutes
Baking time: 45 minutes

Bean and Cheese Enchiladas

1 can (16 ounces) refried
  beans
1 cup coarsely chopped
  onions
1 1/2 cups dairy sour cream,
  divided
1 teaspoon cumin
1/2 teaspoon chili powder
1/8 teaspoon garlic powder
2 cups (8 ounces) shredded
  Wisconsin Sharp
  Cheddar cheese, divided
8 small corn or flour
  tortillas
1 can (16 ounces) enchilada
  sauce
  Lettuce
1/2 cup sliced black olives

Stir together beans, onions, 1/2 cup of the sour cream, seasonings and 1 cup of the Cheddar cheese. Spread about 1/3 cup of mixture down the center of each tortilla. Roll up. Pour a thin layer of enchilada sauce on bottom of 13×9×2-inch baking pan. Place filled tortillas seam-side down in pan. Cover with remaining sauce. Bake in a preheated 350°F oven 15 to 20 minutes. Serve on a bed of lettuce and top with remaining 1 cup sour cream, 1 cup cheese and olives. *Makes 4 servings*

Favorite recipe from **Wisconsin Milk Marketing Board** ©1992

Vegetable-Ricotta Pie

Skillet Pasta Roma

$^1/_2$ pound Italian sausage,
    sliced or crumbled
1 large onion, coarsely
    chopped
1 large clove garlic, minced
2 cans (14$^1/_2$ ounces each)
    DEL MONTE® Chunky
    Pasta Style Stewed
    Tomatoes
1 can (8 ounces)
    DEL MONTE® Tomato
    Sauce
1 cup water
8 ounces uncooked rigatoni
    or spiral pasta
8 mushrooms, sliced
    (optional)
    Grated Parmesan cheese
    and parsley (optional)

Skillet Pasta Roma

In large skillet, brown sausage. Add onion and garlic. Cook until onion is soft; drain. Stir in stewed tomatoes, tomato sauce, water and pasta. Cover and bring to a boil; reduce heat. Simmer, covered, 25 to 30 minutes or until pasta is tender, stirring occasionally. Stir in mushrooms; simmer 5 minutes. Serve in skillet garnished with cheese and parsley, if desired.

Makes 4 servings

Prep time: 15 minutes
Cook time: 30 minutes

Ham and Cheese Casserole

1 package (10 ounces)
    BIRDS EYE® Pasta
    Primavera Style Recipe
    Vegetables in a Seasoned
    Sauce
1 package (8 ounces)
    PHILADELPHIA BRAND®
    Cream Cheese, cubed
$^1/_3$ cup milk
1$^1/_2$ cups (12 ounces) cooked
    cubed ham
$^1/_3$ cup cheese-flavored
    crackers, crushed

Heat oven to 350°F. Cook vegetable mixture, cream cheese and milk in medium saucepan on medium-high heat until cream cheese is melted, stirring occasionally. Stir in ham. Spoon into 1$^1/_2$-quart casserole; top with crackers. Bake 25 minutes.

Makes 4 servings

Prep time: 20 minutes
Cooking time: 25 minutes

Pasta Primavera

1 medium onion, finely
chopped
1 large clove garlic, minced
2 tablespoons butter or
margarine
³/₄ pound asparagus, cut
diagonally into 1¹/₂-inch
pieces
¹/₂ pound mushrooms, sliced
1 medium zucchini, sliced
1 carrot, sliced
1 cup half-and-half or light
cream
¹/₂ cup chicken broth
1 tablespoon flour
2 teaspoons dried basil
1 pound fettucine, uncooked
³/₄ cup (3 ounces) SARGENTO®
Fancy Shredded
Parmesan & Romano
Cheese

In large skillet, cook onion and
garlic in butter over medium heat
until onion is tender. Add
asparagus, mushrooms, zucchini
and carrot; cook, stirring
constantly, 2 minutes. Increase
heat to high. Combine half-and-
half, broth, flour and basil; add to
skillet. Allow mixture to boil,
stirring occasionally, until
thickened. Meanwhile, cook
fettucine according to package
directions; drain. In serving bowl,
combine cooked fettucine with
sauce and Parmesan & Romano
cheese.   *Makes 8 servings*

Pasta Primavera

Bean Soup Santa Fe

1¹/₄ cups dry black beans
 ¹/₂ cup dry pinto beans
 6 cups water
 1 can (14¹/₂ ounces) beef
broth
 1 can (14¹/₂ ounces) stewed
tomatoes, undrained
1¹/₂ cups water
 1 package (1.27 ounces)
LAWRY'S® Spices &
Seasonings for Fajitas
 2 tablespoons LAWRY'S®
Minced Onion with
Green Onion Flakes
 1 teaspoon dry parsley
flakes

In Dutch oven, soak black beans
and pinto beans in 6 cups water
for 1 hour. Bring to a boil; reduce
heat, cover and simmer 1 hour.
Drain beans and rinse. Return to
Dutch oven, add remaining
ingredients. Bring to a boil; reduce
heat, cover and simmer 1 hour.
        Makes 4 servings

Mushroom Frittata

1 teaspoon butter or
   margarine
1 medium zucchini,
   shredded
1 medium tomato, chopped
1 can (4 ounces) sliced
   mushrooms, drained
6 eggs, beaten
¼ cup milk
2 teaspoons Dijon mustard
½ teaspoon LAWRY'S®
   Seasoned Salt
½ teaspoon LAWRY'S®
   Seasoned Pepper
2 cups (8 ounces) grated
   Swiss cheese

In large, ovenproof skillet, melt
butter and sauté zucchini, tomato
and mushrooms 1 minute. In large
bowl, combine remaining
ingredients; blend well. Pour egg
mixture into skillet; cook 10
minutes over low heat. To brown
top, place skillet under broiler 2 to
3 minutes.   *Makes 4 servings*

Presentation: Serve directly from
skillet or remove frittata to serving
dish. Serve with additional Swiss
cheese and fresh fruit.

Hint: Try serving frittata with
prepared Lawry's® Spaghetti Sauce
Seasoning Blend with Imported
Mushrooms.

Tortellini with Three-Cheese Tuna Sauce

1 pound cheese-filled
   spinach and egg
   tortellini
2 green onions, thinly sliced
1 clove garlic, minced
1 tablespoon butter or
   margarine
1 cup low-fat ricotta cheese
½ cup low-fat milk
1 can (6½ ounces)
   STARKIST® Tuna, drained
   and broken into chunks
½ cup shredded low-fat
   mozzarella cheese
¼ cup grated Parmesan or
   Romano cheese
2 tablespoons chopped fresh
   basil *or* 2 teaspoons
   dried basil, crushed
1 teaspoon grated lemon
   peel
   **Fresh tomato wedges for
   garnish (optional)**

Cook tortellini in boiling salted
water according to package
directions. When tortellini is
nearly done, in another saucepan
sauté onions and garlic in butter
for 2 minutes. Remove from heat.
Whisk in ricotta cheese and milk.
Add tuna, cheeses, basil and lemon
peel. Cook over medium-low heat
until mixture is heated and
cheeses are melted.

Drain pasta; add to sauce. Toss
well to coat; garnish with
tomato wedges if desired. Serve
immediately.
     Makes 4 to 5 servings

Preparation time: 25 minutes

*Tortellini with Three-Cheese
Tuna Sauce*

Pineapple Brunch Casserole

Pineapple Brunch Casserole

1 can (8 oz.) DOLE® Crushed
   Pineapple
1 cup biscuit mix
1 cup milk
4 eggs, lightly beaten
6 tablespoons melted
   margarine
1 teaspoon Dijon mustard
$^1/_2$ teaspoon onion powder
   Pinch ground nutmeg
$^1/_4$ lb. cooked ham, diced
1 cup shredded Monterey
   Jack or sharp Cheddar
   cheese
2 DOLE® Green Onions,
   finely chopped

Drain pineapple. Combine biscuit mix, milk, eggs, margarine, mustard, onion powder and nutmeg in blender or beat with electric mixer. Stir in ham, cheese, onions and pineapple. Pour into greased 10-inch quiche dish or deep-dish pie plate. Bake in 350°F oven 35 to 40 minutes or until set.

Makes 6 servings

Prep time: 15 minutes
Bake time: 40 minutes

Acknowledgments

The publishers would like to thank the companies and organizations listed below for the use of their recipes in this book.

Alaska Seafood Marketing Institute
Almond Board of California
Best Foods, a Division of CPC
    International Inc.
Borden Kitchens, Borden, Inc.
Canned Food Information Council
Castroville Artichoke Festival
Checkerboard Kitchens, Ralston
    Purina Company
Clear Springs Idaho Rainbow Trout
Contadina Foods, Inc., Nestlé
    Food Company
Delmarva Poultry Industry, Inc.
Del Monte Corporation
Dole Food Company
Durkee-French Foods, A Division
    of Reckitt & Colman Inc.
The Fresh Garlic Association
Heinz U.S.A.
Kraft General Foods, Inc.

Lawry's® Foods, Inc.
Thomas J. Lipton Co.
McIlhenny Company
Nabisco Foods Company
National Broiler Council
National Live Stock and Meat
    Board
National Pork Producers Council
National Turkey Federation
Norseland Foods, Inc.
Perdue Farms
Pollio Dairy Products Corporation
The Procter & Gamble Company,
    Inc.
Roman Meal Company
Sargento Cheese Company, Inc.
StarKist Seafood Company
Uncle Ben's Rice
USA Rice Council
Wisconsin Milk Marketing Board

Photo Credits

The publishers would like to thank the companies and organizations listed below for the use of their photographs in this book.

Best Foods, a Division of CPC
    International Inc.
Borden Kitchens, Borden, Inc.
Canned Food Information Council
Checkerboard Kitchens, Ralston
    Purina Company
Contadina Foods, Inc., Nestlé
    Food Company
Del Monte Corporation
Dole Food Company
Durkee-French Foods, A Division
    of Reckitt & Colman Inc.
Heinz U.S.A.
Kraft General Foods, Inc.

Lawry's® Foods, Inc.
Thomas J. Lipton Co.
McIlhenny Company
Nabisco Foods Company
National Live Stock and Meat
    Board
National Pork Producers Council
Perdue Farms
Sargento Cheese Company, Inc.
StarKist Seafood Company
Uncle Ben's Rice
USA Rice Council
Wisconsin Milk Marketing Board

INDEX